# HURTING YOUR CHARACTERS:

a writer's guide to describing
injuries and pain from
the character's point of view

## Titles by M.J.

Non-fiction
*The Unofficial Scrivener Workbook*

Fiction
*Changed*
*Indigo Man*
*Disinhibition*
*Engines of Destruction*

## Short stories by M.J.

Ever After - Part of *The Prometheus Saga* anthology
On Dragons Wings - Part of *Dragon Writers* anthology
Three, Two, One, Wake Up - Part of *In Shadows Written* anthology

# HURTING YOUR CHARACTERS:

a writer's guide to describing
injuries and pain from
the character's point of view

BY

## MICHAEL J. CARLSON

ISBN-10: 1545259720
ISBN-13: 978-1545259726


Printed in the United States of America

Book design by Michael Jervis

This is a work of fiction. Names, characters, places, and incidents either are the product of the author's imagination or are used fictitiously, and any resemblance to actual persons, living or dead, businesses, companies, events, or locales is entirely coincidental.

So there.

Cover art courtesy of:
Shutterstock

Cover font: American Typewriter/Bank Gothic
Book Font: Arial/Garamond 11 point

# DEDICATION

To Sparkle, as ever

# Acknowledgments

No one writes a book in a vacuum, and for all those kind souls who offered words of encouragement, suggestions, or just put up with my sustained absences, I thank you. I would like to take a moment to specifically mention my ever-patient beta readers, Laurie Andrews, Cat Lee, Michelle Jefferies, Peter Sartucci, Aaron Fernandez, Lyn Worthen, and Anne Larsen. They read these pages early on, and without their help, there would have been no book. I would also like to mention my Wise Reader and muse, Sparkle. Without her, life would be a pale facsimile.

As always, any errors and omissions are fully my responsibility. Also as always, the reader who finds the greatest number of typographical errors in this book may choose to have a victim named after him or her in a subsequent novel.

# HURTING YOUR CHARACTERS:
a writer's guide to describing
injuries and pain from
the character's point of view

About Pain by Jim Butcher

"Growing up is about pain. And getting over it. You get hurt. You recover. You get over it. You hurt. You recover. You move on. Odds are pretty good you're just going to get hurt again, but each time, you learn something. Each time, you come out of it a little stronger, and at some point you realize there are more flavors of pain than coffee. There's the little empty pain of leaving something behind—graduating, taking the next step forward, walking out of something familiar and safe into the unknown. There's the big, whirling pain of life upending all of your plans and expectations. There's the sharp little pains of failure, and the more obscure aches of successes that didn't give you what they thought they would. There are the viscous stabbing pains of hopes being torn up. The sweet little pains of finding others, giving them your love, and taking joy in their life as they grow and learn. There's the steady pain of empathy that you shrug off so you can stand beside a wounded friend and help them bear their wounds.

And if you're very lucky, there are a very few blazing hot little pains that you feel when you realize you are standing in a moment of utter perfection, an instant of triumph, or happiness, or mirth which at the same time cannot possibly last—and yet will remain with you for life.

Everyone is down on pain, because they forget something important about it: Pain is for the living. Only the dead don't feel it.

Pain is a part of life. Sometimes it's a big part, and sometimes it isn't, but either way, it's part of the big puzzle, the deep music, the great game. Pain does two things: It teaches you, tells you you're alive. Then it passes away and leaves you changed. It leaves you wiser, sometimes. Sometimes it leaves you stronger. Either way, pain leaves its mark, and everything important that will ever happen to you in life is going to involve it in one degree or another."

A special thanks to Jim Butcher for his permission to use this. He really is a good guy under that grumpy exterior.

# Table of Contents

# ONE

## WELCOME TO THE JUNGLE

*Every writer confronted with the dilemma of how severely to hurt a character must understand the consequences of the physical havoc created. Injuries should be realistic, reflect the character of the person inflicting the insult, and be tailored to the needs of the plot. More sophisticated than in the past, today's readers have become avid, critical consumers of media violence. Hence, your story's accidents and injuries and the convalescence they cause must ring true.*
— Introduction to Body Trauma, by David W. Page

What this book is, and isn't—and its *reason d'être*

What this text isn't

This text is not and should not be considered a medical text (although some superficial medical terms and concepts will be discussed at a laymen's level to help with understanding). It isn't a medical reference or a substitute for consultation with a medical professional regarding any personal questions or issues that involve the symptom commonly referred to as pain. This text is not and should not be used as a reference while discussing personal issues or any symptoms with any medical professional, for any reason. Finally, this text is not and should not be considered a substitute for good judgment and common sense. If you are looking for answers to any personal issues regarding the symptom commonly known as pain in this text, you are looking in the wrong place. While those are important issues, they are well beyond the scope of this text. This text is also not an introduction to the external description of trauma and its effect on the body, nor is it an overview of the American medical system or what happens in an emergency room (where I spent a good deal of my youth and later, my career, albeit on different sides of the suture needle). There are already excellent books available on this subject. What we will be covering here is the subjective side of trauma and the resultant

1

pain—the symptoms your character will experience over the course of their relentless torture at your hands as you write their stories.

**What this text is**

This is a reference work for writers. This book is a reference for writers to facilitate causing harm to their fictional characters for fictional purposes and is intentionally written in a humorous tone to make the information more palatable and encourage the more realistic depiction of trauma in fiction. Why, you might ask, do writers need a reference book on human physiology, especially the physiology of injuries and pain? Good question. Many writers, even experienced writers, have a poor understanding of how to describe acute pain from the character's point of view. There are many good reasons for this.

How often have you read a novel where a main character suffers a significant injury, only get up and shrug it off for the remainder of the story. Did that engage you emotionally, or did it pull you away from the story, at least for a few minutes, while you wondered how the character could recover up from being tortured, and still have enough strength to save the day? Does a character in a novel or a movie climbing a cliff with a broken arm bother you? How about a character knocked unconscious for an hour, only to wake up good as new and run around as if nothing happened?

As a child, I loved comic books. I invariably used my entire weekly allowance to buy the latest offering from DC or Marvel. My first crush was on Jean Gray and I wanted to attend Professor Xavier's School. Many of you may have had the same addiction. Some of you may have been introduced to literature in this manner, as I was. If you're writing a superhero tale, you may not need the information contained within this book. After all, Clark Kent has gotten along nicely for seventy years without so much as a stubbed toe. But even the Man of Steel had to interact with Lois and Jimmy. At this point, I'm reminded to mention Man of Steel, Woman of Kleenex (copyright 1971), an essay by Larry Niven covering the physical logistics of a Superman/Lois Lane courtship and mating. Not to be read with a mouthful of any liquid.

# MICHAEL J. CARLSON

People read fiction for two reasons: for entertainment and escape. Entertainment removes us from the usual mundane trivialities or chronic anxieties of day-to-day life. However, I believe fiction not only allows us an avenue of escape but a method of coping with and putting reality into perspective at the same time.

Story concept and writing craft aside, there are two very basic requirements for a fiction story to be engaging: First, there must be conflict. Without conflict, there is no story. At least one that will hold the reader's attention. Second, the reader must either identify with or root for a main character. There are probably exceptions to this rule, but I can't think of any.

Beginning writers are told the mantra, which they repeat faithfully: Hurt your characters, hurt your characters, hurt your characters. But, fortunately for most writers, they've never experienced the kind of trauma that they expect their characters to not only survive but ignore, soldiering on to the eventual confrontation and overcoming of the antagonist. More often than not, in these cases the scene rings false to the reader, deflating the writer's credibility. The connection is broken and the chimera is dispelled, even if only temporarily, revealing the emperor's underpants.

Something writers too often forget is that in the course of hurting their characters, their characters have been injured, sometimes significantly. While inflicting injuries on their characters, the writer may not realize how seriously her characters will be affected by the damage she's dispensed. Those details must be dealt with, same as the clouds above their characters' heads or the grass below their feet. The only way for a writer to convey any of these experiences is by describing them, clearly and effectively. Only then, will the scene ring true for the reader, engaging him or her emotionally and viscerally and pulling them more fully into the story through the character.

Often, writers have difficulty with this area of description because he or she has no direct knowledge of the true extent of the injuries they've inflicted on their characters. How many writers have had broken arms or ribs, or sprained ankles, or concussions? Before you ask, I'm certainly not advocating writers go out and jump off the garage roof in order to understand a broken leg, although it might narrow the field somewhat of competition for my own work. Nor am I offering a weekend S&M getaway for writers, although that might also be fun.

### Raising the Stakes

At last count, I've been reading for the better part of six decades, and I've noticed a shift in storytelling over the past thirty or forty years. Before that time, or in the dark ages, as my younger friends like to say, a story was related to the reader much as it would be if told by a narrator, with the characters kept safely on the other side of the narration (the "fourth wall" in movie terms). Fiction stories were geared toward creating a relationship between the story and the narrator, with the reader being assigned a voyeuristic role.

No longer.

Now readers are exposed to the characters on a much more intimate level. The reader is "pulled into" the story, and sympathizes with the characters. This is the proverbial two-edged sword—while the stories are more exciting (we hope) and a more efficient avenue of escape, writers are pushed to new levels of description to fully convey what their characters are experiencing, and are often presented with the task of describing injuries from their characters' point of view.

Readers of fiction want one thing—a powerful emotional experience. They want and expect to be someone else temporarily. They want to feel something for the characters in whom they are investing their time and attention. Emotion is the common element of all fiction. This is an important concept for the beginning author to understand completely. Readers have no interest in simply reading about someone else having powerful emotions. For a few hours, readers want to live an exciting life facing down international terrorists and solving impossible puzzles. They want the adrenaline rush of living someone else's thrilling, exhilarating life. Without that element, modern readers will become bored.

Imagine if you can, the tedium of spending hours your life watching someone you don't know crying or kissing someone you've never heard of. That's lifeless and insipid. No one has never bought a novel in hopes that would deliver a mediocre emotional experience. Powerful emotions make stories more enjoyable and memorable.

If in the course of engaging your readers at this visceral emotional level, you can (and indeed, should) transport them to a place real enough and introduce them to characters compelling enough that they convince your reader to view their own world through new eyes, you can move mountains. The old saying about the might of the pen is as true today as it ever was. And when we wield that pen, eventually, whether in fiction or in real life someone always gets hurt.

For the unfortunate characters who people our stories, the natural outcome of this particularly dangerous recipe is, as my grandmother used to say, that someone's going to get hurt.

It's true. Writers everywhere are encouraged to hurt, maim, and kill their characters in ever more gruesome and exciting ways and we try, lord knows.

Until now, the only avenues of information writers have had to assist in this challenge are personal experience (ouch), interviewing others who have had the injury (sometimes impossible), or scouring medical texts, that, while accurate, are about as interesting as watching mud dry. Even relying on fellow writers is hit and miss. How are we to know if our favorite thriller or romance author has any idea what a broken arm or a concussion really feels like? Or, more importantly, do they really understand the extent and implications of these injuries? With very few exceptions (and I'm a science fiction fan), a character who jumps out of a helicopter from a hundred feet, lands in a river, swims to shore and walks away as if nothing happened stretches my suspension of disbelief to the point of snapping me entirely out of the story. I believe getting the details right is worth the effort and can often lead to story possibilities I hadn't thought of before.

# HURTING YOUR CHARACTERS

As you read this text, you'll notice words like "probably" and "usually" and "more likely than not" used repeatedly. Those aren't typos, nor are they writing tics. There really is a tremendous variability built into biological systems. The incapacitating pain one character's broken toe causes may allow another character to hobble to safety (or their next injury). This is also a good thing as it allows writers to tailor the injuries they'll inflict on their characters to the character's nature and the needs of the story to some degree.

So, who am I to proclaim expertise on the subject? I'm a medical expert. I graduated from a U.S. Medical school, finished my residency in family medicine, and maintained board certification for sixteen years. Besides practicing family medicine, I worked in emergency departments in both a large, urban hospital and a smaller, rural setting, and literally did thousands of minor procedures in the course of my career. I've also studied the art and craft of writing for the last ten years and have written nonfiction articles, novels, short stories, and have spoken at several writing conventions on this topic.

I also trained and taught martial arts for a decade (I still work out, but I lost interest in tournaments years ago), and have ridden motorcycles for over forty years, so I've had and seen my fair share of injuries.

As with most nonfiction, the suggestions and guidelines in this text are based on the work of some very smart, dedicated, people. If you want to know who most of them are, please check out the References section at the end.

A review of modern sources reveals a scarcity of literature dealing with how to describe injuries and subjective physical pain effectively. I suspect the one underlying reason is that there seems to be no direct neuronal pathway in the brain to connect the experience of pain with the higher centers of the brain associated with speech. That may be why it's so difficult for a person in pain to describe their pain to a caregiver or medical practitioner.

## Conventions
I've used the following conventions throughout the text to make things consistent and easier to understand.

Web addresses appear in:
`courier new`

New terms, especially medical phrases appear in *italics* and are followed by easy-to-understand definitions. Italics is (are) also used to indicate stressed words.

**Bold** indicates keywords or highlights new sections

The English-speaking world is still sorting out the use of generic pronouns. In the past, he was understood to refer to both men and women. Odd, but traditional. Replacing he with they is awkward at best, and often downright silly sounding. So, in an effort to be fair and politically correct, he and she are used in roughly equal numbers.

Because most fiction readers are women, I'll tend to use she when referring to the reader, but don't expect too much consistency here.

The text is a reference and probably shouldn't be read straight through. Especially chapter 2. Tread lightly in there, it's a quagmire.

**Foolish Assumptions**
You want to get published, or you have been published and want to explore the topic on a deeper level and take this area of your craft further. Congratulations on your professionalism.

You're either writing a novel, planning to write a novel, or have written at least one novel. Novels typically run 60,000 words or more—enough room to stretch out and move around a little. Short fiction will, by its nature be more sparse in descriptions. Do not confuse limited space with inadequate description. It's often much harder to describe something in fewer words and still get the point across. The reader is encouraged to encounter some good flash fiction as an example.

# HURTING YOUR CHARACTERS

You understand that fiction is big enough to accommodate many opinions on craft. Hemingway's description of trauma is as spartan as I can imagine, but don't think for a minute that just because he chose to convey his character's injuries through implication and innuendo, he was unfamiliar with them. He was intimately knowledgeable with those injuries through direct personal experience. He had mastered his craft to the point that he could convey meaning between the lines.

## The structure of the chapters

Generally, the chapters will cover the area of trauma in an overview of the common mechanisms of injury, the usual mechanism of the injury (how it most often takes place), the initial symptoms associated with the injury, the typical emotional reaction to the injury, and the expected recovery time(s) for a young, otherwise healthy individual (however else we may differ, men and women are remarkably similar in this respect).

## So, then, what this text (hopefully) offers

It's an effort to give you, the writer or potential writer a superficial handle on the physiology of acute injuries and better tools for the description of your characters' subjective experience of acute pain. It's hopefully a reference for how to write a scene involving an injury more effectively, thereby engaging your readers more fully at an emotional level. And finally, it will try to give an approximate time frame for recovery from common injuries of the type most novelists expect their characters to endure for our reading pleasure. And, hopefully, it'll be fun, as well as informative. Again, I'll try to keep the medical terminology to a minimum, and there's a short dictionary at the back of the text.

This text is about describing the subjective experience of acute pain. Please be aware, we won't be discussing chronic pain. Nor will we be discussing illnesses, like diabetes, heart disease, or autoimmune disorders. If your leading lady needs any of these as a plot device, I'll have to write another book. FYI, several people have suggested including a discussion on anaphylaxis reaction (e.g. to insect stings or certain foods), but I ultimately rejected this for two reasons; while anaphylaxis can be debilitating and can be used as a significant plot device, the mechanism is a reaction to an exogenous (outside) protein, essentially your character's immune system responding to something. Anaphylaxis is also more an example of an illness than an injury for our purposes. Likewise with poisoning. There are many good texts on ingestion of toxic substances, but the symptoms are very substance-specific, and adequately covering the subject could easily end up requiring another whole book.

So, we should get started. Oh, do NOT read the next chapter, unless you're having trouble sleeping. Disclaimer aside, you really should try to understand how things happen in the body, albeit on a very superficial level. If you have a clear understanding of anatomy and physiology, I suggest you just skip to Chapter 3. That's where the fun starts.

# TWO

## HUMAN PHYSIOLOGY FOR WRITERS

CAUTION: THIS CHAPTER MAY CAUSE DROWSINESS

This chapter is the introduction to **Physiology** and **Homeostasis** for writers. It's the chapter for those who insist on getting an intellectual handle on things. Hopefully, that includes everyone. So, let's push off, but we'll try not to get too far from shore.

This chapter lays the groundwork for a necessarily superficial understanding of what goes on inside your character's body. Before we, as writers, can understand and properly convey how our characters experience pain and painful stimuli, and what those experiences mean to them in the context of our plots, we have to first have some understanding of the processes being disrupted. In this chapter, we'll also define some basic terms related to how the human body functions.

### Concepts and Terminology

A comprehensive guide to the anatomy and physiology of pain—not. Believe it or not, this is meant to be an overview. To that end, I'll endeavor to keep the minutiae down to a minimum and try to keep explanations as real-world as possible. I promise to keep it as basic as I can, and I'll use common terms and analogies whenever applicable.

Pain can be either physical or emotional. But even a purely physical sensation usually has an emotional component attached to it, so we'll look at them separately. But first, we need a baseline for our discussion. Specifically:

## What's Normal...?

For a normal, reasonably healthy adult the following findings are "normal." Some variation is usual and what's normal for one person may be abnormal for another.

Pulse rate between 60-100 beats per minute. A fitter person will have a rate towards the slower end of the margin and a child or young person will have a naturally higher rate. Any drastic increase or decrease in pulse rate is usually a cause for concern.

Blood pressure 90-140 over 60-90. This can vary with the time of day, the amount of stress, and a number of other factors. High blood pressure is not usually immediately dangerous but can cause long term damage. Low blood pressure can cause faintness, dizziness, and blackouts and is usually a sign that there is an underlying problem to be treated. The higher number (the systolic blood pressure) is the pressure associated with the heart's contraction, and normally 90 mmHg (millimeters of mercury) is the minimum to maintain blood flow to the brain and hence consciousness. The second number (the diastolic pressure) is the general pressure in the circulatory system between beats, and 60 mmHg is considered the minimum to maintain blood flow to the heart (the coronary arteries only perfuse the heart during relaxation). Gee, that was simple. Right?

Body Temperature 36°C (96.8°F) to 37.5°C (99.5°F). Relatively minor variations in temperature outside that margin are cause for concern. Trivia fact: few people actually have a body temperature of 98.6°F. This temperature was arrived at by convention (common agreement) because it's a nice, round number in the metric system (37°C). The average oral temperature for most people is actually between 97.9 and 98.2°F, but that converts to 36.6 to 36.8°C.

# HURTING YOUR CHARACTERS

Let's start at the beginning. No, not all the way back to the Big Bang, but with one of the most basic concepts—the idea that the human body strives to maintain a **dynamic equilibrium**. Dynamic equilibrium is a lot of syllables to convey a simple concept: the body actively does things to keep itself in its comfort zone. Think of this as sweating when the temperature becomes too warm or shivering when it becomes too cold, even if the temperature change is from eating or drinking something too hot or cold.

A good question to ask here is: why does the body do this? Wouldn't it be simpler to move into the shade on hot days on lay on a flat rock in the sun to warm up? Short answer—yes. Long answer—no, because we, like all the other mammals, just aren't built that way. We're warm-blooded. This means that we have internal control mechanisms to react to our environment. This is a good thing generally, as many of the reactions that take place at a cellular level can only happen within a narrow range of conditions. The reason for this is most, if not all of the chemical reactions that happen inside us are helped along by things called enzymes. I know you've heard that word before, and now you know what enzymes do—they speed up chemical reactions inside the body so that those reactions can take place in a reasonable amount of time even though the enzyme itself isn't changed in the process.

The downside of having to rely on enzymes to keep things happening is that when we go outside set parameters (like temperature or blood pH), the enzymes don't work as well. If we get too hot, the enzymes lose their shape and stop working at all, too cold, and they slow down, if the pH (acid-base balance) goes too far out of whack, the enzymes can fall apart. All this chaos results in progressively bad things for us, until, at some point, we cease to continue to function at all if the proper balance isn't restored. That would be coma leading to death and is definitely in the bad column for your character. That's why people start to behave strangely (or at least more strangely than usual) if they're exposed to extremes in temperature, chemicals, toxins (like alcohol), or lack of oxygen.

The body's ability to maintain this "just right" zone is called:

# MICHAEL J. CARLSON

**Homeostasis**

Homeostasis (noun) ho·me·o·sta·sis is defined in Steadman's Medical Dictionary's 27th edition as; 1. The equilibrium (balance between opposing pressures) in the body with respect to various functions and to the chemical compositions of fluids and tissues. 2. The process through which the equilibrium is maintained. This is an important basic concept in that the body is not a static device, but a constantly changing, highly complex series of sensors, processes and feedback mechanisms, all involved in maintaining a properly balanced environment consistent with life and comfort. In simpler terms, the body tries to do whatever it takes to maintain the best comfort zone for its occupant—your character. Whenever this balance is upset, the body will attempt to correct the imbalance.

At the most basic level, the organs most directly responsible for maintaining this balance are the brain (through the *hypothalamus*, the autonomic nervous system, and the endocrine system), the liver and the kidneys.

The hypothalamus is a portion of the brain that contains a number of small brain cells with a variety of functions. One of the most important functions of the hypothalamus is to link the nervous system to the endocrine system. What that means is that it is the link between your character's "fight or flight" response and the surge of adrenaline that pushes up her heart rate, allowing her to outrun the dinosaur or the antagonist's henchmen. It's located in an area of the brain roughly straight back from the bridge of the nose to the intersection of a line drawn between and about two finger widths above the openings to the ears. In other words, in just about the geographic center of your character's head. In humans, it's roughly the size of an almond. It's responsible for certain processes and activities including control of body temperature, hunger, thirst, fatigue, sleep, and body functions related to the time of day.

The liver is responsible for metabolizing toxic substances (like that beer or glass of wine your character had with dinner) into forms that the body can handle of and maintaining carbohydrate metabolism (things like turning the carbs in the pasta your character had for dinner into more usable forms (like glucose or blood sugar) that he or she can use to outrun the antagonist until act three.

The kidneys are responsible for the excretion of wastes, regulation of blood pH, re-absorption of substances into the blood, and regulating blood water levels by maintaining the correct salt and ion levels in the blood.

What does that mean for the leading lady in your novel?

It means that we (and your character, unless she is of reptile or amphibian ancestry) must maintain a near-constant body temperature. Drop the temperature a few degrees, and chemical reactions inside the body slow down and eventually stop. Lower the body's temperature some more and blood vessels in the arms and legs close off, keeping the blood's warmth close to the organs necessary for life. This is why your character's fingers and toes will turn white when she's exposed to that blizzard. Lower the temperature further, and water inside the cells starts to freeze and expand (ice takes up more volume than liquid water), resulting in cell death and what we normally call frostbite.

Ouch.

Speaking of ouch, some people just have to have a big, new shiny word to toss around at their next party. Here it is; *nociception* (soft C for each). It means "the perception of physical pain." And that's enough of that.

**Pain**
What is pain?
The "standard" definition of pain is that of the International Association for the Study of Pain:

"An unpleasant sensory or emotional experience associated with actual or potential tissue damage, or described in terms of such damage. Pain is always subjective. Each individual learns the application of the word through experiences related to injury in early life. It is unquestionably a sensation in a part of the body, but it is also unpleasant, and therefore also an emotional

experience."
(IASP. Pain 1979(6)249-252, ex Shipton, 1993).

Wow, that was a mouthful.
For our purpose, we can shorten the definition a little. Pain, especially acute pain, is an unpleasant experience. We don't like it and we don't want to repeat the experience under most circumstances (you S&M types and Country & Western music lovers, put your hands down).

## Skin

Here's something that I was shocked to discover: Men and women view skin differently. I know it shouldn't have caused a moment's hesitation, so different are our other thought processes, but it did, and there's nothing for it but to explain. If you already know this one, just drop to the next paragraph. Men (typically) view skin as a barrier between them and the outside world. This is what's taught in medical and nursing schools, where the emphasis is on keeping germs out and body fluids in. But guess what? It's a male thought process. Women (typically) view the skin as a sense organ through which they experience the world. Isn't that a beautiful, poetic way of looking at it?

It's also something we can use to our advantage if we can understand the implications. The same exquisite sensitivity that sends an electric sensation through us at the gentle touch of a loved one can be used to cause tremendous amounts of pain to our characters. The word "exquisite," by the way, is defined as intensely felt, and is used in medical texts to describe both extremely painful and extremely pleasant experiences.

Skin is both a resilient barrier and a wonderful sensory organ. It will be used in both capacities later in the book. It contains several types of **receptors** that recognize different stimuli and are sensitive to light touch, heat and cold, and vibration. For our purposes, receptors are a nerve ending sensitive to external stimuli and able to transmit a signal to a sensory (afferent) nerve. We'll mostly be concerned with the General Somatic Afferent nerves (GSA) and General Visceral Afferent nerves (GVA). Examples of Specialized Somatic Afferent nerves (SSA) are things like vision, hearing, and balance. Smell and taste are examples of General Visceral Afferent nerves (GVA).

The obvious question, for our purposes, is: what kinds of sensations does skin convey? Generally, the good stuff, like very well localized (specific to a couple of millimeters) light touch, mild heat and cold, and painful stimuli. There's a biological advantage in skin carrying localized sensations. This means your character is able not only to distinguish between a touch on the shoulder and on the hand but should be able to feel two separate sensations if they are more than about half a centimeter from each other (about half a finger's width). The individual advantage to this is that skin is fully capable of alerting us to sensations as fine as a butterfly's touch, as tiny as a needle's point, and temperature changes of a few tenths of a degree. It alerts us to the impact of the outside world upon us for good or ill as well as protecting us from it.

So, to get back on track then, how does the skin send sensations to us?

To understand the mechanisms by which your characters experience acute pain, we have to discuss some complex ideas, at least on a superficial level. I've made every effort to translate the sometimes complicated concepts into layman's terms and use everyday words and analogies. You'll notice I've used the terms "acute pain" and "pain" interchangeably in this text. There's a reason for that. Acute pain has survival value, both for our species and for your character (e.g. causing her to remove an injured limb from a harmful stimulus), but chronic pain is of little or no use, except as a plot device. Therefore, describing the experience of chronic pain is of little concern to most beginning writers and beyond the scope of this text.

This section outlines the basic anatomy and physiology of acute pain. It's boring and tedious, and while I've made every effort to replace the two-dollar medical geek terms with something a little more down-to-earth, it's not entirely possible. When I had to leave the multi-syllabic terms in, I've tried to give real-world interpretations and analogies to help your understanding. I hated learning this in school. I'm relatively certain it'll bore you to tears, but it will give you a basic understanding of what's happening in and under your character's skin so we can go on.

I like to use the wiring analogy when talking about nerves. This is a hold-over from my days of studying wiring diagrams of cars and motorcycles as a teenager. Why I was studying wiring diagrams as a teenager isn't important right now, except that it's where my analogy comes from.

All nerve impulses travel at a lot less than the speed of light we're used to in computers. The speed of nerve impulses is more along the lines of meters per second. There are two good reasons for this; one is that nature didn't have rolls of copper wire lying around during the evolution of the nervous system, and two; it's a system that grows with the organism, using similar mechanisms to those it already uses for other processes, instead of trying to build wire of copper, atom-by-atom. And it works okay for the needs of almost every living animal on the planet. Next time you stick a needle in your finger see if it's not a pretty quick way of moving impulses around.

### The Peripheral Nervous System

This is the network of nerve cells that surround and interact with every part of the body, no matter how small. These nerve fibers carry sensation toward or away from the Central Nervous System (CNS), and are separated from it by microscopic gaps (synaptic clefts). The two systems are different in that in some cases the peripheral nerves can regenerate (regrow) after injury while the central nervous system can't.

For our purposes, nerves conduct impulses in one direction or the other, but not both. The ones that conduct toward the brain are **Afferent** or sensory nerves, the others are called **Efferent** or motor neurons, resulting in movement. So, a primary afferent neuron carries an initial stimulus toward the brain, away from the injury and the efferent motor neuron carries the order to move the affected body part away from the painful stimulus. Got that? Good.

### Acute pain

Acute pain is a physiological response to stimuli that are damaging or potentially damaging to normal tissue. This pain begins suddenly and is usually, but not always, sharp in quality. It serves as a warning of physical damage to the body. It might be mild and last for moments, or severe and last for days or weeks. In most cases, acute pain, by definition, lasts less than three months and gradually disappears when the underlying cause has been removed, either by treatment or because it has healed.

There are four basic processes involved in the perception of pain. These are;

**Transduction** (or "jangling the nerve-endings," usually at the skin or someplace similar);

**Transmission** (just what it says—getting the impulse of pain from one place to another);

**Perception** (this is the "ouch" portion of the impulse, where it's actually felt as an unpleasant sensation);

**Modulation** (damping down the impulse to allow the system to reset). Modulation is also a mechanism by which large numbers of brain cells can be activated together by a chemical *neurotransmitter* dumped into the surrounding space. A neurotransmitter is just what you'd expect, a chemical produced by the body that results in a response in the adjacent nerve fiber(s).

For our purposes, there are two types of nerve fibers. There are several other kinds of nerve fibers, but these two are the ones we're interested in. Let's call them A-delta fibers and C fibers. We could call them anything, including Mickey and Pluto, but let's use the names those really smart, very unimaginative physiology people gave them, so we're all talking about the same things.

*Myelin* (you'll see that again, later) is a wrapping around the A-delta nerve fiber kind of like insulation around regular wires. In this case though instead of color-coding and keeping things from shorting out, myelin helps move impulses (like pain or pleasure) through the nerve at a faster rate. It's made from cholesterol and just one of the reasons why "100% fat-free" shouldn't apply to humans.

## Transduction of pain

Transduction begins when the free nerve endings of C fibers and A-delta fibers of primary afferent neurons respond to painful stimuli. These nerve endings are exposed to painful stimuli when tissue damage and inflammation occurs as a result of, for example, trauma, surgery, inflammation, infection, and the like.

The pain receptors are cells that respond to potentially damaging stimuli by sending signals to the spinal cord and brain. These receptors are distributed in the *somatic* structures (skin, muscles, connective tissue, bones, and joints) and *visceral* structures (organs, such as the heart, stomach, liver and the gastrointestinal tract). This process, called nociception, is cell receptors reacting to chemicals indicating trauma, which allow positively and negatively charged particles, normally on opposite sides of nerve cell membranes, to freely flow in and out of the cell, sending the impulse along the nerve fiber to the brain, where neurotransmitters are released, causing the perception of pain in sentient beings. Neurotransmitters are chemical messengers, made by the body, which some cells can release and thereby stimulate other cells in specific ways. Mostly, for our purposes, neurotransmitters carry chemical messages across a synaptic gap or junction from one nerve cell to another (e.g. the gap between presynaptic and postsynaptic nerve cells).

## Primary afferent nociceptors

Claudia Cheng

Updated in August 2006

"Primary afferent nociceptors are specialized free nerve endings of primary afferent nerves (A-delta and C fibres). They are generally the first structures to be involved in the nociceptive process and are located in various body tissues including skin, muscle, connective tissue, blood vessels and thoracic and abdominal viscera. The skin is supplied by A-delta and C-nociceptors/fibres. Muscles, joints, fasciae and other deep somatic structures are supplied mainly by C- but also some A-delta nociceptors/fibres.

"A-delta nociceptors are activated by mechanical and thermal stimuli. A-delta fibres are the smallest of the myelinated nerves. They are 2-5 um in diameter and are fast with a conduction velocity of 6-30 m/s. Activation of A-delta fibres results in short-lasting, pricking-type pain

"C nociceptors are polymodal (mechanical, thermal, chemical). C-fibres are unmyelinated, less than 2 um in diameter and have a slow conduction velocity of 0.5-2 um/s. Activation of C fibres results in dull, poorly localized, burning type pain

"Stimulation of these nociceptors occurs when the pain threshold is reached. This then results in propagation of impulses along the afferent fibres toward the dorsal horn of the spinal cord (periphery) or to the medulla (cranial). Stimulation of the primary afferent nociceptors which result in pain can be from
1)   physical stimuli - mechanical injury, noxious heat, radiation
2)   byproducts of tissue damage resulting in release of cellular contents and mediators from the nociceptive afferents. Chemicals released from damaged cells include bradykinin, potassium, serotonin, histamine, cytokines, nitric oxide, hydrogen ions, prostaglandins, leukotrienes, slow reacting substance of anaphylaxis. Mediators released from the afferent nociceptors include substance P, calcitonin-gene-related peptide, neurokinins.

"After a brief period of noxious stimulation, peripheral sensitization occurs. This is a normal physiological response to pain. The mechanism involves release of intracellular contents from damaged cells and inflammatory cells, collectively known as the "inflammatory soup." In the presence of this "soup," the sensitivity of the primary afferent nociceptors is increased, there is lowered threshold to stimulation and there is prolonged and enhanced response to the stimulation. Clinically, this is manifested as primary hyperalgesia."
- Claudia Cheng August 2006
http://www.aic.cuhk.edu.hk/web8/primary_afferent_nociceptors.htm

The A-delta and C fiber fibers are associated with different qualities of pain. These are listed below.

# MICHAEL J. CARLSON

**Characteristics and functions of A-delta and C fibers:**

## A-Delta fibers
Characteristics:
Primary afferent fibers (carry sensation from the injury to the brain)
Myelinated (wrapped with lipid insulation to speed up the transmission of impulses)
Larger diameter than the C-fibers below (although they're the smallest myelinated nerves)
Fast conducting

Receptor type:
High-threshold mechanoreceptors respond mechanical stimuli over a certain intensity.
Pain quality:
Polymodal—respond to more than one type of noxious stimuli, i.e.:
- Mechanical (direct pressure)
- Thermal (heat)
- Chemical (acid/base, toxic substance, *ischemia*, or lack of blood and oxygen, and infection)
Well-localized
Sharp
Stinging
Pricking
Referred to as 'fast' or 'first' pain

## C fibers
Characteristics:
Primary afferent fibers (carry sensation from the injury to the brain)
Small diameter
Unmyelinated (lack the wrapping that speeds up transmission of impulses)
Slow conducting

Receptor type:
Polymodal—respond to more than one type of noxious stimuli, i.e.:

# HURTING YOUR CHARACTERS

- Mechanical (direct pressure)
- Thermal (heat)
- Chemical (acid/base, toxic substance, *ischemia*, or lack of blood and oxygen, and infection)

Pain quality:
Diffuse
Dull
Burning
Aching
Referred to as 'slow' or second' pain

So, as you can see from the lists above, A-delta and C fibers are built very differently. This is good, as they do different things. Remember above, when I mentioned that myelinated nerve fibers sling painful sensations upstream pretty quickly as these things go? That's the A-deltas. Now look at the sensations they carry; quick, sharp, stinging, well localized (meaning you can point to the place with a finger). What does the term "high-threshold" mean, you ask? It means the stimulus doesn't hurt, doesn't hurt, doesn't hurt, until pow, it hurts. Then it really hurts. A good example is that same sewing needle; it's just pointy until you jab it home, then... ouch! As an aside, this is why a very small diameter needle introduced at a slower rate (like an acupuncture needle) doesn't hurt (much)—it slides between nerve endings and doesn't set off many when it does hit one or two.

How about those C fibers? Dull, aching, burning, poorly localized pain. Sound familiar? Should. This is what your characters will feel when the quick, sharp pain fades. This is also what innervates organs inside the body, which is why your characters can't always point to where that appendicitis or heart attack hurts with just one finger.

Keep in mind, as noted above, that there's also overlap; some C fibers innervate the skin along with A-delta nerve fibers, and deep tissues receive some innervation from A-delta nerves.

## Noxious (painful) stimuli and responses

There are three categories of painful stimuli:

1. **mechanical** (direct pressure, swelling)
2. **thermal** (burn, scald)
3. **chemical** (acid/base, toxic substance, ischemia, or lack of blood and oxygen, and infection)

The cause of stimulation may be internal, such as pressure exerted by an alien trying to burst out of your character's chest or external, like a burn. This painful stimulation causes a release of several chemical mediators from the damaged cells.

These chemical mediators activate and/or sensitize the pain receptors to the painful stimuli. This results in an action potential and generation of a pain impulse. Or, in regular terms:

Nerve impulses, all nerve impulses, are a combination of electrical and chemical processes. Impulses travel along a nerve because little, tiny holes that are usually closed to positively and negatively charged sodium and potassium particles in the nerve's covering (membrane) and keep them on either the inside or the outside suddenly open, allowing these ions to flow in or out, as the case may be. This propagation of the impulse travels along the nerve in this manner, from one end to the other, like a wave. When the impulse has moved on, little pumps move the ions back to their respective sides of the membrane in preparation for the next nerve impulse.

## Transmission of pain

The transmission process occurs in three stages. The pain impulse is transmitted from the site of transduction along the appropriate nerve fibers to the spinal cord, from the spinal cord to the brain stem, and through connections between the thalamus, cortex and higher levels of the brain.

There's a short separation between the terminal ends of both the A-delta and C fibers and the dorsal horn of the spinal cord. In order for the pain impulses to be transmitted across this gap to the dorsal horn, excitatory neurotransmitters are released, the names of which are well beyond the scope of this explanation. Just take it on faith, that some really smart people spent a lot of grant money to find and name these (okay, they didn't really spend much time or money naming the things, but you get it).

There is a chemical called "substance P" (the "P" stands for, you guessed it, pain) which is synthesized within the central nervous system and whose function seems to be to sensitize the brain to new painful stimuli in the setting of existing long-standing pain. The reason for this substance seems to be pretty straightforward: a brain that is exposed to constant pain may become dulled to new pain input. It's the job of substance P to make it possible for the brain to be alerted to a new injury. The downside is that once your character starts circling this particular drain, it'll take a while for his brain to down-regulate the production of substance P.

In terms of pain perception, thresholds for feeling pain are remarkably constant from individual to individual. i.e. peripheral receptor stimulation of sufficient intensity will reproducibly cause pain at the same level in most normal, healthy people. This is the reason nerve conduction studies yield so much valuable information. The response of the individual and his tolerance of pain will differ markedly between individuals.

Analgesic drugs that act peripherally include non-steroidal anti-inflammatory agents, corticosteroids, local anesthetic agents, and even novel drugs such as substance P antagonists (One such antagonist that does NOT appear to work very well is capsaicin, but opioids, serotonin antagonists, baclofen, and clonidine may also inhibit substance P release).

### Perception of pain

Perception of pain is the end result of the neuronal activity of pain transmission and where pain becomes a conscious multidimensional experience. This multidimensional experience of pain has affective-motivational, sensory-discriminative, emotional and behavioral components.

The pain impulse is then transmitted from the spinal cord to the brain stem and thalamus by two main ascending pathways. Again, the names are less important that the fact that they exist. Okay, so now the pain stimulus has reached the brain, where it can be turned into the "ouch" portion of the program. The brain doesn't have a specific pain center, so when impulses arrive, they are directed to multiple areas in the brain where they are processed.

These areas are:
The *reticular* system is responsible for the physical response to pain and for warning the individual to do something, for example, automatically removing a hand when it touches a hot saucepan. It also has a role in the affective-motivational response to pain such as looking at and assessing the injury to the hand once it has been removed from the hot saucepan.

The part of the brain called the *somatosensory* cortex is involved in the perception and interpretation of sensations. It identifies the intensity, type, and location of the pain sensation and relates the sensation to past experiences, memory and cognitive activities. It identifies the nature of the stimulus before it triggers a response, for example, where the pain is, how strong it is and what it feels like.

The *limbic* system is responsible for the emotional and behavioral responses to pain, like attention, mood, and motivation, and with processing pain and past experiences of pain (the "damn it" part).

**Modulation of pain**
The modulation of pain involves changing or inhibiting transmission of pain impulses in the spinal cord. There are multiple, pathways involved in the modulation of pain. They're referred to as the descending modulatory pain pathways (DMPP) and can lead to either an increase in the transmission of pain impulses (excitatory) or a decrease in transmission (inhibition).

An excitatory postsynaptic potential (EPSP) is an electrical potential that makes the postsynaptic neuron more likely to fire a signal. This most commonly occurs because of the release of neurotransmitters, the most common of which is glutamate, into the tiny space separating the presynaptic (PNS) and postsynaptic (CNS) nerve fibers.

Descending inhibition involves the release of special chemical neurotransmitters that block or partially block the transmission of pain impulses, and therefore produce a reduction of pain. Inhibitory neurotransmitters involved in the modulation of pain include opioid-like substances (enkephalins and endorphins) and several others that are made normally in the body (opium and morphine and all the opium-based street drugs work because they're similar to things the body normally makes). So, why would the body make things that deaden pain? Good question.

Other than the initial, quick jerk to remove the injured body part away from the stimulus, acute pain tends to be paralyzing. The more painful the stimulus, the more paralyzing it can be. Internal pain modulation is important to allow the higher levels of the brain to function to get us away from the painful stimulus.

Also, after that first quick jolt of pain, the continued sensation can make it impossible to feel any new injuries. This dampening down of the initial sensation helps to reset the system to allow for new stimuli to alert us of any additional injuries. Clever, don't you think?

A good bit of the above description was taken almost verbatim from: http://www.anaesthetist.com/icu/pain/Findex.htm#pain_how.htm

With appropriate and (hopefully) helpful simplification. I've made every effort to convey the original meanings and concepts as I understand them, and of course, I apologize to those authors for any misunderstanding on my part.

There's more.

**Peripheral receptors**
There's an additional phenomenon at play, called "First pain" and "Second

pain." Let's spend a moment on those. The idea here is fairly straightforward; when most people do something silly, say, cut their finger, they get an immediate jolt of sharp pain at the site. This is "first pain." However, after a few seconds, when that sensation dies off, they notice a second, duller, more diffuse sensation at the site. This is "second pain" coming on.

First pain is described as sharp, and "pricking." It localizes to a well-defined part of the body surface. The receptors for this first pain are high threshold mechanoreceptors. There appear to be specific "nociceptors" which mediate pain and ONLY pain.

Second pain is due to stimulation of receptors that exist in many tissues (but not in, paradoxically, the brain). It is often described as dull (i.e. not sharp) and aching. It's poorly localized. Receptors for this second pain are termed polymodal nociceptors. This pain tends to last beyond the acute painful stimulus. Sources, pathways, perception of and treatment of the two types of pain are very different. Visceral pain (pain felt in the internal organs, like the heart or gallbladder) is predominantly of the "second pain" type.

Interestingly, visceral pain is also referred to a region of the body surface specific to that organ (for example, the famous "left arm pain" with heart attacks or pain below the shoulder blade in cases of gall bladder problems). Most organs have these corresponding "referred pain" areas and they're well-known in medicine.

### Neural pathways
"First pain" responses are conveyed from the periphery to the dorsal horn of the spinal cord in small myelinated fibers (A-delta) while "second pain" is conveyed in non-myelinated C fibers. This is important, especially when considering the "gate control theory" detailed below. Also of importance to this theory are afferent stimuli coming in via large myelinated fibers (A-beta fibers), from peripheral vibration/pressure/touch receptors.

Neurogenic pain, originating in damaged or abnormal C fibers, may respond to membrane- stabilizing drugs such as anticonvulsants (e.g. carbamazepine).

# HURTING YOUR CHARACTERS

The *spino-reticulo-diencephalic* system is rich in opiate receptors, while the spinothalamic tract has very few. This explains why opiates (e.g. morphine) have good analgesic properties for visceral pain without affecting pinprick sensation.

Spinal pathways: local interconnections. There are several. Of great importance are connections mediating so-called "gating." The basic idea here is that "painful stimuli" coming into the cord on C fibers can be modified by other inputs, which "close the gate on the incoming pain." These inputs come from:
A-delta fibers; A-beta fibers; and others.

This arrangement has several practical consequences:
*Transcutaneous Electrical Nerve Stimulation (TENS) works
*Dorsal column stimulation (DCS) works
*Acupuncture works
*Rubbing the skin locally helps decrease pain

**The response to pain**
Responses to visceral pain are very different from those evoked by somatic pain. Somatic pain is a fancy way of saying "of or pertaining to the body, more specifically the muscles and bones." Visceral, or organ pain, generally results in tonic muscular spasm (decreasing movement of the affected area), e.g. stomach or intestinal pain usually results in involuntary tightening of the abdominal muscles. Somatic pain usually causes withdrawal of the affected part of the body "to protect this region from further damage." As already mentioned, the sensations reported for the two pains are also quite different.

We're all also aware that pain (be it somatic or visceral) can have profound autonomic effects. Some of the reasons for this have been alluded to: there is a good degree of cross-over between the somatic and visceral systems at the level of the spinal cord and also extensively at higher centers, with projections to, for example, the hypothalamus. Also of note is the close relationship between sensory afferents and sympathetic outflow (Cross, 1994), e.g. pain will cause your character to perspire, her heart to speed up, and her pupils to dilate.

**Objectively measuring pain:**
Objective measurement of pain may be within our grasp in the not too distant future. The gene c-fos, for instance, is rapidly expressed in the spinal cord in response to painful (but not to other) peripheral stimuli. This gene is evidence that we should not rely only on pain being "always and only subjective." Pain is also something that can now be documented in a fairly objective fashion, albeit only using fancy tools in the laboratory. But pain doesn't stop there. As Cross [1994] said:
"The affective-motivational aspects of pain originate in the periphery, and suffering is not merely a matter for the neocortex; it is profoundly more ancient and primitive phylogenetically and is reflected in fiber tracts and neural networks throughout the nervous system."

What that means is that pain has been with us for a long time, and its physical reality is reflected in measurable, chemical changes as well as perception. After several millennia of searching, we're on the verge of understanding how pain works on a molecular-chemical level. Pretty exciting.

**A brief note on opiates and their receptors**
There are three main types of opioid receptor: delta, kappa, and mu. All of these are widely distributed in the brain and are not only concerned with modulation of pain perception, but also with a variety of other functions. This explains why in trying to control pain, we encounter many unwanted side-effects. For example, mu receptors are widespread in the brainstem *parabrachial nuclei* (where stimulation of them causes respiratory depression), and dependence may be related to receptors in the *locus coeruleus* and ventral *tegmentum*. Some have asserted that mu1 and mu2 receptors are mainly concerned with pain and respiratory depression, respectively, but this is too simplistic.

The different levels of these substances also helps to explain the wide variations in the perception of pain in different people. Natural internal opioids are found throughout the central nervous system (CNS) and prevent the release of some excitatory neurotransmitters, for example, substance P, therefore inhibiting the transmission of pain impulses.

Opioids work in two main ways: they either block neurotransmitter release (by inhibiting calcium influx into the presynaptic terminal) or hyperpolarize neurons by opening a potassium channel (and therefore effectively temporarily knock the neuron out of action).

When considering the effects, and by extension, the resulting symptoms of trauma, the way to think of the action is as a transfer of energy. This is true, no matter the specific type of trauma. Without jumping too deeply into physics, the prospect of which I'm sure will excite all fiction writers, let's just say that the force of the trauma on your character is equal to the mass of the object delivering the blow multiplied by the speed that object is moving when it contacts you leading man/woman. There, that wasn't so bad, was it?

Let's move on to stuff that's a little more fun.

If all this wasn't enough for you, here's some references & further light reading:

Richardson, BP. Ann NY Acad Sci 1990 (600) 511-519. Serotonin and Nociception.

Cross, SA. Mayo Clin Proc1994 (69) 375-383. Pathophysiology of Pain. This article on pain mechanisms is still by far the best summary we have encountered!

Helme, RD. et al. Medical J. Australia 1990(153)400-406. Neural Pathways in Chronic Pain.

Mansfield MD. et al. BJA. 1996 (76) 358-361. Influence of dose and timing of administration of morphine on postoperative pain and analgesic requirements.

# MICHAEL J. CARLSON

Editorial. BJA. Jan 1996 76(1) 1-4pp. An article on the significance of c-fos. Well worth reading.

Shipton, EA. Pain, Acute & Chronic. W.U.P.1993 (ISBN 1-86814-241-8). Reading this book gives one a great understanding of pain.

Hamill, RJ & Rowlingson, JC. Handbook of Critical Care Pain Management. McGraw-Hill. 1994. (ISBN 0-07-025814-7).

See [Cervero, F. Physiological Rev 1994(74.1) 95-129pp] for a review of the sensory innervation of the viscera.

# THREE

## MINOR INJURIES

*"I'll have you know that I stubbed my toe last week while watering my spice garden, and I only cried for 20 minutes."*

— SpongeBob SquarePants, *No Weenies Allowed*

**Minor Injuries**

Bumps, bruises, scratches, cuts, and grazes are all inconvenient but not incapacitating. Most of the things listed here would be considered minor inconveniences for your character at most. The important thing that a minor injury can do for your story and character is to show a certain amount of physical vulnerability. Superman, for instance, has never experienced a bump, bruise, a cut finger, or most of the things that humanity shares. The true superhero character has no more in common with the other characters in the story or the reader than Data, the android from the Star Trek series. In that respect, the superhero character becomes a fantasy story.

Physiologically, superheroes are characters resembling the old gods; Apollo, Zeus, Athena, Aphrodite, Mercury, Poseidon, Loki, and Thor. In the case of Thor and Loki, they made it into the comic books. Superhero-type characters in literature share common characteristics with these ancient characters: they're fallible, powerful, and strive to maintain an affable relationship with humanity. Even the archetype "heroes" from Greek mythology, e.g. Ulysses, Jason, Hercules, etc., exhibit many of the same vulnerabilities as everyday people. By and large, demigods are typically a pretty selfish bunch, often with certain antisocial tendencies, who often happened to be descendants of gods.

But enough philosophizing. Let's get back to having some fun torturing our characters.

Minor injuries are an excellent plot device for injecting some humanity into your characters, temporarily debilitating them, or giving a necessary plot twist to a story that is becoming predictable, all without the potential risk of stretching your reader's suspension of disbelief to the snapping point. Minor injuries may require one character to suddenly need the assistance of another, changing the group dynamic. They may also place a major character in an unexpected position of vulnerability to antagonistic forces, increasing tension. Finally, they may add some reader sympathy toward the antagonist of the story, making that character seem more real for the reader.

So, what exactly are we talking about when we use the term "minor injuries?"

### Abrasions

Abrasion (scrape) - An abrasion is a wound caused by superficial damage to the skin, no deeper than the epidermis. It is less severe than a laceration and bleeding, if present, is minimal. Mild abrasions, also known as grazes or scrapes, do not typically scar horribly, but deep abrasions may lead to the formation of scar tissue. A more traumatic abrasion removes all the layers of skin is called an avulsion.

Abrasion injuries most commonly occur when your character's exposed skin comes into moving contact with a rough surface, causing a grinding or rubbing away of the skin (think "road rash").

Abrasions, like burns and frostbite, are graded according to severity. The first-degree abrasion involves only an epidermal injury, and behaves similarly to a burn, both in the sensations generated for your character and in the time it takes to heal. This is especially true because part of the damage done to the skin by an abrasion is, in fact, a burn because of the friction of the skin against the rough surface.There is almost no bleeding associated with a Grade 1 abrasion. The other consideration, even in superficial abrasions, is that debris may be deposited in the area and may be a source of infection.

# HURTING YOUR CHARACTERS

**Avulsion**

An avulsion injury is one in which a body structure is forcibly detached (except for arms or legs, that's referred to as traumatic amputation and there's nothing minor about that). Superficial avulsion injury most commonly refers to layers of skin which have been torn away, exposing underlying structures, similar to but generally more serious than abrasions. Also, while the term abrasion implies applied friction between moving surfaces, avulsion implies more of a tearing motion. And, yes, it's every bit as painful as it sounds.

The mechanism of an avulsion injury can be as varied as the imagination, everything from a section of skin caught in and torn away in some sort of machinery to the purposeful removal of a victim's skin (Buffalo Bill from *Silence of the Lambs*).

This type of injury is responsible for massive injury to the superficial nerves and intensely painful as air contacts millions of tiny, traumatized, severed nerve endings per square inch. Some specific types of avulsion injuries have descriptive names as a shorthand method of describing the trauma, i.e. "degloving" is just what it sounds like; the skin of the hand and possibly part of the forearm is ripped off the arm. I bet you're thinking of that scene in the Terminator movie. Don't try it at home, kids. This is discussed more in-depth in Chapter 7.

The pain associated with this type of injury is usually described as "screaming pain" because that's what the victim does. The pain is immediately and totally debilitating, often sufficient to cause the victim to pass out. The sensations associated with this type of injury are often described as an "overwhelming searing, ripping or burning sensation followed by an intense, unremitting, throbbing ache.

The only way this injury can heal is by; a) surgically reattaching the skin and hoping the nerves and blood vessels reattach, b) surgically amputating the affected area, or c) an incredibly long, painful process where the limb is allowed to form scar tissue to replace the lost skin, usually accompanied by infection without immediate intensive care.

## Traumatic nail avulsions

Trauma to a finger or toenail can cause the nail plate to be torn away from the nail bed. Unlike other types of avulsion injuries, nails are rarely reattached. Following this type of injury, the exposed nail bed quickly forms a germinal layer which hardens to protect the tender tissue until the nail regrows. Typically in young, otherwise healthy people, fingernails take 3 to 6 months to completely regrow, while toenails may require 12 to 18 months. Likewise, similar to injuries on the face, hands, and especially the fingertips are packed with extraordinarily dense numbers of sensory nerves. Traumatic removal of a fingernail is described in medical texts as "exquisitely" painful, described as an intense, searing, ripping or burning sensation followed by a throbbing ache. That's why it's such an effective torture device. If you doubt my word on this, just read almost any prisoner of war novel set in Southeast Asia.

## Traumatic tooth avulsion

Finally, the word avulsion is also used to describe the tooth that is completely or partially detached from its socket. If your character loses a tooth, usually because of some sort of trauma, i.e. a punch, kick, car crash, etc., reimplementation can reasonably be attempted for approximately one hour or so after the injury. This kind of injury would be expected to be associated with a sharp pain from the impact, followed by throbbing, local to the missing tooth's socket, sometimes radiating to most of the face or head.

## Fingertips

In rock climbing, if a small section of skin is torn loose from the fingertips, it's called a "flapper." This usually is the result of friction between the climber's fingers and the handhold if the climber slips. Usually, this is a quick, ripping pain, followed by an intense, throbbing ache.

## CONTUSIONS
### Ecchymosis (shallow bruise)

An example of a contusion would be a blow to a bony part of a limb or a joint, the head, or the body (usually the rib cage). It hurts a lot at the time of impact and may swell and stiffen (as anyone who's banged their shin will attest), but rarely causes any significant damage to your character or major disruption to the story. The impact may also have the effect of temporarily disrupting the 'power supply' to the limb meaning the person getting hit is likely to lose their grip on anything they're carrying and be unable to move the extremity for a few seconds to a few minutes (think "funny bone" here).

In this type of injury, smaller blood vessels are usually damaged by the impact, allowing blood to seep into the surrounding subcutaneous tissues under the skin. As a type of *hematoma*, a bruise is always caused by bleeding into the interstitial spaces. However, the term "contusion" implies trauma, either accidental or with intent, as in "intent to do harm." Trauma sufficient to cause bruising can occur from a wide variety of situations, including car crashes, falls, and physical attacks. In medical terms, a contusion implies an "impact-type trauma not severe enough to cause an underlying fracture."

Subjectively described, contusions usually begin with a sharp, stinging or jarring pain, localized to the point of impact on your character's skin. From there, your character will probably experience a dull, aching, throbbing pressure-type sensation that may be moderately debilitating out of proportion to the seriousness of the actual injury.

### Hematoma (deep bruise)

A hematoma (a collection of blood) is a localized collection of blood outside the blood vessels, usually in liquid form within a body part, that causes a painful swelling. This distinguishes it from the more superficial ecchymosis, which is the simple spread of blood under the skin in a thin layer. Both are commonly called a bruise. Hematomas may occur due to overexerted or overstretched muscles in the arm or leg, or even spontaneously if a blood vessel bursts. For our purposes, though, most hematomas and ecchymoses are synonymous with bruises. They are most commonly the result of an application of the proverbial blunt object that does not result in a laceration (see Contusion above).

Hematomas can form anywhere but often occur within a muscle. Other times hematomas can form into hard masses under the surface of the skin, most commonly the scalp after a mild head injury. If the hematoma is caused by the application of blunt force, your character will experience a deep debilitating pain at the impact site or if the cause is a torn muscle, a deep ripping sensation. After the initial injury, the steady, achy pain associated with their formation is caused by the limitation of the blood leakage into a subcutaneous or intramuscular tissue space. This is also a key anatomical feature that prevents such injuries from causing massive blood loss. When enough blood seeps into a space, the resultant pressure will stop further bleeding. A hematoma will typically cause your character decreased movement of the extremity due to a dull, achy pressure and physical limitation because of contraction of the muscle due to the size of the hematoma.

Your character can, however, be harmed by a hematoma. In moderate to severe bruising, your character might experience significant accumulation of blood combined with localized swelling that produces a situation known in medical terms as "compartment syndrome." In compartment syndrome, swelling cuts off blood flow to the tissues causing severe pain, inability to move the extremity, and potentially limb threatening loss of blood flow past the swelling. Depending on the location and size of the hematoma, it could potentially produce a life-threatening situation for a character.

Hematomas in a joint can reduce mobility of the extremity and present roughly the same symptoms as a fracture. In most cases, gentle movement and exercise of the affected muscle after a period of rest and elevation is the best way to introduce the collection back into the blood stream.

Bruises can take anything from a few seconds to over a day to appear and anything from a day to several weeks to completely fade away again. Soft fleshy areas typically bruise much more colorfully. In most cases, the sac of blood or hematoma eventually dissolves. Or, they may continue to grow or show no change. If the hematoma does not disappear in a week or two, it may need to be surgically removed.

The slow process of reabsorption of hematomas can allow the broken down blood cells and hemoglobin pigment to move in the connective tissue. For example, a patient who injures the base of his thumb might cause a hematoma, which will slowly move all through the finger within a week. Gravity is the main determinant of this process.

### Excoriation (scratch)

In common with Abrasion, this is caused by mechanical destruction of the skin. The difference is that an excoriation is a focal loss of (usually) the top layer of skin caused by scratching, scraping, or gouging. Excoriations are usually linear and may be self-inflicted (by scratching too vigorously) or from an external source (e.g., brushing/rubbing against a sharp surface like sea shells, coral, thorns, or metal) that produces one or more (again, usually) linear, superficial marks on the skin.

An excoriation refers to any scratch or shallow cut on the skin. Certain skin diseases, such as dermatitis and eczema, can cause the skin to form raised, itchy areas or lesions and result in excoriations from scratching. Finally, there are psychological conditions that can lead a person to intentionally scratch his or her own skin, creating cuts and abrasions. Simple excoriations sting. They are easily treated and usually heal quickly, rarely becoming infected or leaving scars.

An excoriation is commonly caused by physical means. This could be the fingernails, a sharp object or a rough surface. An excoriation is different from an open wound because the damage or degradation is restricted to the surface of the skin and doesn't routinely penetrate deep enough to cause serious bleeding.

If an excoriation becomes deep enough, it is more properly described as an abrasion or avulsion.

### Incision (cut)

A sharp, linear wound, made into a body tissue or organ, like with a knife or scalpel during surgery, by accident, or intention. By definition, incisions almost always extend through the dermal layer of the skin into the subcutaneous tissues, requiring stitches (sutures) to aid in proper healing. There are 3 major reasons for suturing deep lacerations or incisions: to decrease pain. As mentioned above, when nerve endings are exposed to air, it changes their pH causing a sensation of pain. When the skin's integrity is restored, the pH typically returns to normal, reducing pain. Also, suturing aids in the reduction of infection by closing bacterial access to the interior of the body. Finally, suturing aids in wound healing by leaving the body with a smaller defect to repair.

Since we're talking about it, to answer the age-old question, yes, sutures are the same thing as stitches. Here's where the confusion lies: traditionally, "stitches" were something a seamstress did, while "sutures" were what surgeons did. Really, it's that simple. Technically, suture material can be any of several substances, including (not surprisingly) thread (either natural silk or any of several man-made polymers). However, they can also be made of animal tissue ("gut" sutures), stainless steel (staples), in some cases, cyanoacrylate (Dermabond/super glue), but "stitches" implies knots, which require thin, flexible material. There are advantages and disadvantages to each that are well beyond the scope of this book. For the sake of ease, we'll choose to use the more commonplace "stitches" to cover the lot.

The rule of thumb about stitches is that if your character can separate the edges of the wound, look in and see the icky parts underneath the skin (fat, muscle, or bone), the wound should probably have stitches.

**Laceration (tear)**
An irregular wound caused by blunt impact to soft tissue overlying hard tissue or tearing. In some instances, this can also be used to describe an incision. Lacerations may be of almost any severity, from minor injuries that heal spontaneously to major, significant injuries that will require medical treatment for your character (please refer to Chapter 6 for the more serious end of the spectrum).

A superficial laceration is a cut or tear of the skin that has not extended below the epidermis (the outermost layer of skin). A paper cut would be a good example of this. Most of the time, your character will experience a small amount of bleeding, with sharp, fairly intense, well-localized pain out of proportion to the severity of the injury itself. Superficial lacerations can be short or long, but cannot expand into the dermis, which is the layer of skin below the epidermis, and therefore do not require stitches.

As noted above, the reason lacerations and incisions hurt regardless of the severity of the injury is that when the integrity of the skin is separated, nerve endings are severed and exposed to the air, which has a drying effect changing the pH of the nerve. It is that change in pH that causes the nerve stimulation that results in your character's sensation of pain. That's why, the more jagged the edges of the laceration are, typically, the more it will hurt.

**Puncture wound**

Puncture wounds are caused by objects that penetrate the skin and possibly the underlying layers, such as a nail, needle or knife. For a discussion of more serious puncture wounds, please jump to Chapter 7.

Small, clean, superficial puncture wounds usually do well. Even small puncture wounds may be very tender because, as noted earlier, the skin carries most of the sensory nerves. Puncture wounds are typically described as discrete, "pointed," prickly, sharp, or stinging sensations that will immediately get your character's attention.

Minor puncture wounds can occur anywhere and almost anything can be responsible (many plants, as well as man-made artifacts, have very pointy parts). Often, especially when dealing with plants, the puncture wound may become irritated or infected because of toxins that the plant has evolved over time to defend itself, compounding your character's problems.

What your character needs to do about a puncture wound is dependent upon the material that punctured the skin, the location, depth, timeframe, footwear and underlying health status of the character. Punctures in the bottom of the foot, especially the joint area at the toes may be of higher risk of bone and joint involvement. Children brought by a parent and adults with an on-the-playground injury tend to seek help earlier and thus have a lower incidence of infection than escaped convicts on the run through a swamp with dogs and a trigger-happy sheriff close behind. After 24 hours without proper treatment, your character may have an early infection. Unsuspected fragments of sock or rubber sole are a major source of potential infection when the puncture wound in on the bottom of the foot (as in, the nail your character stepped on as she was sneaking through that abandoned construction site to plant a homing device on a henchman's car).

A puncture to the foot can represent a unique challenge to your character. When the foot is punctured, the skin acts as a spatula, cleaning off any loose material from the penetrating object as it slides by. This debris often collects just inside the puncture wound which then acts like a trap door holding it in. Left in place, this debris may lead to infection, either as cellulitis (a diffuse, red, tender area of swelling) or an abscess (a discrete, painful, closed sac of pus). Clean removal of the wound edges with a pointed blade allows for the removal of debris and the unroofing of superficial small foreign bits of dirt and junk found beneath the foot's thick skin surfaces.

Puncture wounds can also be an effective means of torture if your character is into that sort of thing. Small diameter implements can be used to pierce the skin with the effect of being very painful, depending on the area of skin chosen, doesn't destroy skin like burning, heals quicker than cutting, doesn't form scar tissue rapidly. It can be used repeatedly in the same area without fear of desensitization, and it's relatively safe, in that it's difficult to accidentally do enough damage to kill a prisoner by poking them with needles.

## Crush Injuries

A crush injury is a form of blunt trauma. It occurs when a force or pressure is put on a body part, usually over a fairly large area, although your character hitting his thumb with a hammer qualifies. This most often happens when a part of your character's body is squeezed between two heavy objects, e.g. the proverbial rock and a hard place, or that landslide of gold coins as they race away from the grumpy, annoyed dragon.

Most often accidental, crush injuries can be responsible for broken bones, bruising, bleeding, lacerations, and in some cases, something called compartment syndrome. Compartment syndrome is a potential complication of crush injury. It's defined as increased pressure in one of the body's Compartments which contain muscles and nerves (usually in an arm or leg). The mechanism involves severe swelling in an extremity after an injury or significant overuse, which causes insufficient blood supply to the muscles and nerves within the compartment.

So, how does a crush injury feel? Depends. Depends on the amount of weight and the body part involved. A wheelbarrow-full of beach sand dumped on your character's legs will feel entirely different than a Volkswagon on his chest. The beach sand on the legs will be minimally bothersome other than an inability to move the affected part. A car, even a compact car, on your character's chest will have more far-reaching effects.

While a little outside the realm of "minor injury," the initial sharp pain of a serious crush injury might be followed by numbness, tingling, and paresthesia ("pins and needles" sensation). Moderate to severe crush injuries often result in deep, constant, poorly localized pain. A severe crush injury can also result in fracture, laceration, nerve injury and potentially a secondary infection.

# FOUR

## HEAD INJURY–STARTING AT THE TOP

Neurologist: "I want you to repeat after me Though they had, bad disguises, it was their inscrutable style that allowed them to escape the dogged policemen." Matthew: "Though they were bad guys... bad, bad, bad guys... they... sc... scre... screwed... the pp... policemen... dd... doggy style?... That can't be right. Let me try again." Neurologist: "No!"

So, someone's decided to bash your main character over the head with something blunt. Ouch.

Head injury refers to trauma of the head including the scalp, face, and skull and may or may not include injury to the brain. Other terms, including traumatic brain injury, head trauma, and concussion are often used interchangeably in literature.

Head injuries are probably the most common injury in fiction, and probably the most commonly misrepresented injury as well. A character may be noiselessly silenced or incapacitated by a single blow to the head as is done to the redoubtable Stephanie Plum in *Three To Get Deadly* and *High Five* by Janet Evanovich with no discernible after-effect. The character will invariably recover completely unless the plot requires amnesia. In reality, this is probably the least reliable method of rendering someone unconscious. Any head injury significant enough to cause loss of consciousness may be serious enough to cause intracranial bleeding (subdural or epidural hematoma), skull fracture, blindness, or death.

A Mayo Clinic researcher, Eelco Wijdicks, M.D. and his son, Coen recently conducted a study of 30 movies released from 1970 to 2004 that contained actors depicting comas that ranged from a few days to as long as ten years. They evaluated the accuracy based on the appearance of the patient, complexity of care, accurate cause of coma, probability of awakening, and appropriate compassionate discussion between the physician and family members. They found that in most cases, patients portrayed in movies did not have feeding tubes, contractures, or tracheostomies (that's a hole in the throat placed by a skilled surgeon to allow breathing and safe feeding of a comatose patient). Patients depicted also remained in a "normal, muscular tone, and perfectly groomed appearance," which Dr. Wijdick says trivializes prolonged coma to simply a 'sleeping beauty' state of sleep. In the majority of the films analyzed, physicians caring for comatose patients were poorly represented as "cavalier, sarcastic, detached or uncompassionate." Finally, the researchers found that 28 of the 30 movies analyzed portrayed inaccurate, miraculous awakenings—often over seconds and as if from a terrible nightmare—with no cognitive defects or other long-lasting effects from the coma, sometimes after years.

Dr. Wijdick's concern lies primarily in the 2nd aspect of his research. When the same scenes were shown to 72 nonmedical viewers and revealed that the majority of lay viewers could not identify inaccuracies in 36% of the scenes depicting coma.

A concern expressed by Matthew Colebeck, a graduate student at the University of Sheffield, UK, who is working on his doctoral thesis on depictions of coma and brain injury in literature, is that the consistent inaccuracies and misrepresentations of head injuries and coma are "creating a fictional science instead of writing science fiction."

### Mechanism of Injury

There are essentially two basic mechanisms of survivable head injury your characters may experience; closed head injuries and penetrating injuries. A closed head injury is where the dura mater lining inside the skull remains intact. The skull could be fractured, but not necessarily. An open head injury is one where the lining inside the skull has been breached. A penetrating head injury occurs when an object pierces the skull and reaches or penetrates the dura mater. Brain injuries may be diffuse, occurring over a wide area, or focal located in the small, specific area.

In the first, more common injury, your character will either be struck by some object (club, candlestick, etc.). This is called a direct injury. Or the character might strike an object and bounce off, going on to strike yet another object, i.e. an automobile crash, where the character's head strikes the steering wheel, dashboard, or airbag and then bounces off, to strike the head restraint part of the seat (personal peeve here—the car seat's headrest was not designed to rest the head against, but originally designed to prevent whiplash-type neck injuries in car crashes. Head rest is an abbreviation for head-restraint). This is referred to as a coup-countercoup injury, and the second impact usually results in more diffuse damage than the first. A third type of closed injury is rotational, and usually comes from a blow to the side of the face that causes the head to turn on the axis of the neck (i.e., if your character is clocked on the jaw in the ring or by an evil-doer).

Penetrating head injuries are less common than closed head injuries (outside of wartime experiences) and result in an approximately 50% mortality rate. The primary mechanism of injury in penetrating head trauma is from direct damage to the brain from the object and the associated bleeding. Penetrating trauma can either result in very localized damage (as in the case of an ice pick or knife blade), or relatively diffuse injuries, as in the case of gunshot wounds where the shock wave from the missile can be very destructive.

I realize that was a lot of information to digest in a few paragraphs and at first glance, you may ask yourself "so what?" The above concepts may be helpful to you and your writing in the future. Go back quickly and make sure you understand them. That knowledge may help you understand what you've inflicted on your character or open up new ideas in your fiction.

Facial injuries and fractures typically result from a blunt object (fist, stick, rifle stock, etc.) striking the face and penetrating the soft tissues, potentially affecting the eyes. This type of injury usually causes some degree of disfigurement as the facial bones tend to be delicate.

# HURTING YOUR CHARACTERS

Facial bruising is actually quite uncommon. It takes quite a hard blow or a blow that impacts with the soft tissue around the eyes to leave a mark. However, when such a blow does land, bruising can be pronounced, because of the amount of blood flow to the head. This increased blood flow is the reason minor cuts and lacerations on the scalp and face bleed out of all proportion to their seriousness. It's also why cuts and lacerations to the head heal more rapidly than the same injury on another part of the body. About twice as fast, by the way.

Lastly, a more subtle type of head injury is oxygen deprivation. This can occur from any number of causes, like asphyxiation (Chapter 6) or severe blood loss causing shock (Chapter 9). A particularly good portrayal of this type of injury was given by Harrison Ford in "Regarding Henry."

## GENERAL OVERVIEW OF HEAD INJURIES
### Minor Head injuries
The human skull is pretty robust and evolved to take a fair amount of punishment. Consequently, the occasional bump won't do all that much damage. A minor bump on the head may leave a character feeling dazed and suffering from a headache, blurred vision and ringing ears but will clear within a few minutes.

### Medium Head Injuries
A more forceful blow (equivalent to a fall of several feet) can lead to complications of the injury. Concussion (damage to the brain tissue) is quite common after a hard blow to the head and is often accompanied by temporary unconsciousness (and it should be very temporary if you don't want your character to be permanently damaged). This can also result in dizziness, especially when standing up, nausea and, not surprisingly, a nasty headache.

### Severe Head Injuries
A blow to the head resulting in prolonged unconsciousness will almost certainly result in some brain damage, possibly a fractured skull and bruising or bleeding within the brain itself. It can be fatal either straight away if the

damage is extensive enough or later as the blood from the injury causes pressure on the brain. The pain from such injuries would have most characters unable to concentrate on much else.

## Head Injury Symptoms
Headache
Confusion, disorientation, memory loss
Dizziness (the feeling that the room is spinning), vertigo (a tilting or falling sensation), unsteadiness
Nausea, vomiting
Feeling of the skin "crawling" or a tingling sensation, or a "muffled" sensation, like being "packed in cotton"
Pupils uneven in size and/or reaction
Blurred vision, double vision, or seeing bright lights
Sluggish reactions, sleepiness
Ringing or buzzing in the ears

Impact on other characters: Someone suffering from a suspected head injury should be watched for at least 24 hours, and woken every few hours if they're asleep, to check for the above symptoms or changes in mental abilities.

Classification: No single definition of concussion, mild head injury, or mild traumatic brain injury is universally accepted. According to the classic definition, no structural brain damage occurs in concussion. It is a functional state wherein symptoms are caused primarily by temporary biochemical changes taking place at the cell membranes and synapses.

In 1993 the American Congress of Rehabilitation Medicine defined mild traumatic brain injury as 30 minutes or less of loss of consciousness, 24 hours or less of posttraumatic amnesia and a Glasgow Coma Scale score of at least 13 pretty normal findings based on response to visual, auditory, and movement stimuli. Other definitions of concussion incorporate focal neurologic deficit and altered mental status in addition to amnesia and the Glasgow Coma Scale.

# HURTING YOUR CHARACTERS

Side note: the Glasgow Coma Scale is the accepted standard by which unconscious people are evaluated. It assesses eye response, verbal response, and motor response to various stimuli, assigning numbers 1-6 to each. The worst findings, like "no eye opening, makes no sounds, and makes no movements" even in response to painful stimuli would be a GCS 3 (pretty bad stuff). In fact, a GCS 3 with no heart beat or respirations is dead, so, yeah, pretty bad. Less than 8-9 total is severe, and 13 or above is considered minor.

Grading system: Concussion (mild head injury) is typically broken into 3 grades. The 3 most commonly used grading scales were developed by Robert Cantau, the Colorado Medical Society and the American Academy of Neurology. While similar, there are subtle differences between the 3 scales.

Specific head injury and problems that may be associated with each:
Generally speaking, Grade 1 concussions are the most common. Grade 1 concussion is what is commonly referred to as "having one's bell rung" or "seeing stars." In movies, this is where we see cartoon birds circling the victim's head. There is no loss of consciousness (LOC) associated with this level of injury in any grading scale and it can be associated with short (<30 minutes) amnesia or confusion, although usually isn't. This is usually the kind of head injury your character would expect to experience at a football game or around the house that causes an expletive.

The lower end of this injury is about as bad as your heroine standing up in the kitchen and bumping her head on an open cabinet door, with nothing more than an "ouch, damn it" moment. At the higher end of Grade 1, she will probably experience headache and may develop nausea, possibly with vomiting, disorientation, and dizziness. These symptoms will resolve in less than fifteen minutes.

A Grade 2 concussion is a little more serious. Your character will still experience no loss of consciousness, but may well have some degree of confusion or post-traumatic amnesia (loss of memory of the incident that is usually temporary but can be permanent), typically lasting from 30 minutes to 24 hours.

She will probably experience the same sort of symptoms as in a Grade 1 concussion, but by definition, these symptoms will last longer than fifteen minutes for your character and should resolve in less than twenty-four hours. At the upper end of Grade 2 injuries, you character may feel "strange," have recurring headaches, be forgetful, or have significant mood swings. These symptoms clear up within three months, by definition.

A Grade 3 concussion is more serious, still. Your character's Grade 3 concussion will have a loss of consciousness associated with it (anywhere from seconds up to five minutes, depending on the grading scale used), and typically associated with some period of amnesia, usually less than 24 hours.

Not much fun, but neither are they the stuff of intense drama. Now, let's see what your main character can expect in the way of symptoms.

**Physical symptoms**
Headache is the most common mild head injury symptom your character can expect. Other symptoms noted above can include dizziness, vomiting, nausea, lack of motor coordination, difficulty balancing, or other problems with movement or sensation. Visual symptoms she may experience include light sensitivity, seeing bright lights, blurred vision, and double vision. Tinnitus, or a ringing in the ears, is also commonly reported.

In one in about seventy concussions, concussive convulsions occur, but these seizures that take place during or immediately after the concussion are not the same as post-traumatic seizures, and they, unlike post-traumatic seizures, aren't in themselves predictive of post-traumatic epilepsy, which requires some form of structural brain damage, not just a momentary disruption in normal brain functioning. Concussive convulsions are thought to result from temporary loss or inhibition of motor function and are not associated either with epilepsy or with more serious structural damage. They aren't associated with any particular long-term effects and have the same high rate of favorable outcomes as concussions without convulsions.

# HURTING YOUR CHARACTERS

## Cognitive and Emotional symptoms

Cognitive symptoms your character might encounter could include confusion, disorientation, and difficulty focusing attention. Loss of consciousness may occur but is not necessarily correlated with the severity of the concussion if it is brief. Post-traumatic amnesia, in which the person cannot remember events leading up to the injury or immediately after it, or both, is a hallmark of concussion.

Other cognitive symptoms can include temporary changes in sleeping patterns and difficulty with reasoning, difficulty concentrating, and difficulty performing complex everyday activities (for instance, your character might be able to drive a car, but might not be able to remember how to get back home).

Confusion is another concussion hallmark, and may be present immediately or may develop over several minutes, but rarely longer than that. Your character may, for example, repeatedly ask the same questions, be slow to respond to questions or directions, have a vacant stare, or perceive other characters' speech as slurred or incoherent. Your character may experience changes in hearing—sounds could be perceived as muffled or sharp, or sensations—they may feel like they are packed in cotton or may even become hypersensitive, with skin sensations becoming "prickly."

Affective results of concussion include irritability (being annoyed by events or sounds that wouldn't normally be bothersome), loss of interest in favorite activities or items, tearfulness, and displays of emotion that are inappropriate to the situation. Common symptoms in concussed children include restlessness, lethargy (excessive sleepiness), and crankiness, difficulty thinking clearly, headache (usually early on), fuzzy or blurry vision (usually early on) irritability, sleep disturbance (sleeping more or less than usual), feeling slowed down, nausea or vomiting (usually early on), dizziness (usually early on), sadness, difficulty concentrating, sensitivity to noise or light, balance problems with standing or walking, being generally more emotional than usual, difficulty remembering new information, feeling tired, having no energy, or excessive nervousness or anxiety. Any of these symptoms, but most commonly, dizziness and headache will get worse when your character tries to sit up or stand.

Any of the symptoms your character experiences will start immediately after the injury. That means your leading man won't start having severe headaches or dizziness six months after a mild head injury. Symptoms in Grade 1, 2, and 3 concussions usually resolve within a day or two at most. In rare instances, for some people, symptoms can last for days, weeks, or longer, but even in those individuals, symptoms will almost certainly resolve in less than three months. In general, recovery may be slower among older adults, young children, and teens. Those who have had a concussion in the past are also at risk of having another one and may find that it takes longer to recover if they have another concussion.

## Moderate head injury
A little more serious that a mild head injury, this involves a documented loss of consciousness for more than five minutes but (usually) less than an hour and/or a period of traumatic amnesia for up to a week. So, for instance, if your character is hit on the head and wakes up to the police standing over him, or is knocked unconscious and a week later realizes he only remembers flashes of the previous week, he's had a moderate head injury.

What does all this mean for your character? He will probably have any or several of the symptoms mentioned above. Often, the symptoms will persist for a longer time, up to six months in some cases, and may be more intense. On rare occasions at this level of injury some symptoms may last for up to a year or two, and in very rare cases, may be lifelong. Usually, in the instances where a symptom or symptoms are ongoing, there has been some structural damage at the time of the injury, either from a skull fracture, or bleeding inside the skull (referred to as a "closed head injury" in medical circles). Let's take these additional problems in no particular order.

## Skull fracture
Is just what it says; a disruption of the integrity of one or more of the bones making up the skull. Usually, this is synonymous with the term "depressed

skull fracture," but not always. The problem with a skull fracture, even one that isn't severe enough to cause a depression is that, by its nature, the skull is a very robust structure. Any blow with enough force to cause a fracture will also transmit enough force to cause damage to the brain inside. The most common resulting problems have to do with bleeding or swelling, as there's no place for blood or excess fluids from swelling to go. These are:

*Epidural hematoma*—bleeding between the skull and the dura mater (a thin covering surrounding the brain). Usually, this involves rapid bleeding, causing the dura mater to rip away from the inside of the skull (yeah, rip is a good word here, because it hurts like crazy). The bleeding happens because as the dura rips away, it tears small arteries feeding it and the surface of the brain, causing bleeding until such time as enough pressure builds up to stop the bleeding. This occurs just after enough pressure has built up to force the base of your character's brain out through the little hole through which the spinal cord exits (called the foramen magnum). You guessed it, this almost always results in a painful death for your character, as in excruciatingly painful, followed by loss of consciousness and death as the body's basic life support (heart rate and blood pressure control) goes haywire.

*Subdural hematoma*—bleeding below the dura mater which may develop slowly over hours. This is the head injury every ER doc fears. Your character typically gets whacked on the head and loses consciousness for ten or fifteen minutes, and wakes up with a mild headache that may even clear up. He (almost always a he) decides not to go to the ER "because it doesn't hurt all that much anymore," and six or eight hours later, lapses into coma and dies in a day or two.

I've only seen one of these in my career. It occurred in Miami, where I went to medical school. I was volunteering in an ER in the wake of hurricane Andrew. A man's wife brought him into the ER against his will because "he wasn't acting right" after part of his roof fell on him during the storm. His only symptoms were being "spacey" in that his responses seemed slower than one might suspect and his pupils were different sizes. Fortunately, he listened to his better half that night and was in surgery within an hour. He survived, and with timely care, went on to recover with no lasting neurologic deficits.

*Cerebral contusion*—a bruise of the brain itself. Significant, not so much because of direct structural damage to the brain or surrounding tissue, but because of the swelling from the injury. Just as your character's arm will swell if she bumps it against something hard, like the club your antagonist is swinging, when the brain is bumped, it will swell. As a rule of thumb, the harder the blow, the more swelling (again, just like her arm). This swelling can cause the base of the brain to be squeezed out through that same little hole we talked about above, causing that same coma and death.

## Severe head injury

Also known as deep do-do. Your character has come about as close to death as she can get and still draw a breath. You as the author should be aware that damage to the central nervous system is usually permanent. The brain and spinal column do not heal, outside of science fiction or fantasy. If you are sadistic enough to inflict this kind of injury on your character, this is what they can probably expect:

There will be structural damage. This kind of damage would be a depressed fracture or a penetrating wound (like from a gunshot, shrapnel from an explosion, or a sharp implement, such as an ax). Your character will spend at least a week in a coma, usually an induced coma in an intensive care unit of a hospital until the swelling goes down, probably have multiple surgeries to repair damage, and can expect to spend months in a rehabilitation facility, learning how to do things like feed himself, walk and talk again, may possibly never fully recover, and may still die.

This poor creature will likely have severe, lancinating (meaning sharp, stabbing or piercing—feeling sort of like jamming a spike into your character's head) headaches, seizures, or difficulty concentrating. He may be unable to feel or move body parts, or he may have personality changes upon awakening. He will probably have difficulty speaking, may have lost a sense or two (commonly vision, smell or taste), and usually needs help to make it through the day to some degree. Before you start jumping up and down and shouting "yes, yes!" and planning your super villain as a recovered severe head injury patient with a convenient savant quality to crack into the FBI or CIA computers, you should be aware—probably not. Think "stroke" symptoms. This kind of injury wouldn't be expected to leave a character with some new, added ability—that's the stuff of comic books, which is all right, but be aware before hand.

Just sayin'.

**Expected recovery times**
For a Grade 1 concussion: within five to ten minutes would be expected. Your character can expect a full recovery and may feel a little silly for having bumped her head.

Any symptoms associated with a Grade 2 concussion should clear up within a few minutes to an hour or so, and leave your character with no long-lasting residual problems.

Ditto for Grade 3 concussion, except that your character's symptoms may persist for up to three or four months, and in rare instances may take up to six months to clear completely.

Moderate head injury is the gray area where your character's recovery can go almost anywhere. Your character will most likely recover fully from this kind of injury eventually, but it likely won't be easy or quick.

Severe head injury represents a serious, significant trauma to a human being. Always. For Star Trek fans, think Captain Christopher Pike, for everyone else, think walkers, and wheelchairs and difficulty speaking or understanding sentences, depending on the location and extent of the injury. The most common lasting effect of severe head injuries is cognitive impairment. Short and long term memory problems, difficulty with simple math problems, slurred speech, and sentence structure difficulties are common. Physical residuals might include tremors, balance difficulties, and incoordination. For an excellent portrayal of recovery from a severe head trauma, the reader is referred to "The Three Shirt Deal," the seventh book in the Shane Scully series, by the late Stephen J. Cannell.

### Recurrent head injury

The mechanism of injury of multiple minor head injuries over a prolonged period hasn't been well studied and isn't well understood. The preponderance of data assessing the impact of repetitive head injuries on short- and long-term neurologic (cognitive) performance has mostly been focused on the sports of boxing and American football.

In those studies, professional boxers have shown that repeated brain injury can lead to chronic encephalopathy, termed dementia pugilistica, also known as "punch drunk," often resulting in problems similar to severe head trauma above. Likewise, the autopsies of 2 former professional football players with a history of multiple concussions demonstrated changes that were consistent with chronic encephalopathy. So, recurrent head trauma can add up for your characters (I'm looking at you, Travis McGee).
http://emedicine.medscape.com/article/92189-overview

For the reader interested in a more scholarly discussion of head injury and coma in literature, please consider *Waking Is Rising And Dreaming Is Sinking: The Struggle For Identity In Coma Literature* by Matthew Colbeck, PhD. The work explores the representation of coma in fiction and non-fiction and is the result of Dr. Colbeck's thesis. I highly recommend it.

As a last word, I would be remiss to ignore a particularly odious form of brain injury: Shaken Baby syndrome. This injury occurs as a result of violence perpetrated on the most helpless members of a culture and usually results in extensive, permanent brain damage to the victims. Those unfortunate few who do regain some consciousness and grow to adulthood would be expected to experience paralysis of one or more extremities and trouble with cognitive skills, including memory, the ability to learn new information, speech, and understanding written material.

# FIVE

## SPINAL CORD INJURY

**Spinal cord trauma**

I'm aware paralysis can be a difficult subject matter for some and that portions of the information contained within this chapter may be disturbing for readers. My intention is certainly not to be unnecessarily sadistic or coldhearted, but too often in literature, and in movies and television, we are exposed to blatant "Hollywood Healing" that's completely unrealistic.

Normally, once a character based in reality suffers a spinal cord injury, their functional losses will remain even after their other injuries have healed. There are conditions under which spinal cord injuries can be temporary, and I will explain these at the end of the chapter. They may be of considerable use to authors to provide their characters with a "weasel clause" to allow recovery from what would normally be a lifelong handicap. I also realize that in modern America, the word "handicap" is considered politically incorrect. My use of the word here is in its denotative context only with no value judgment attached, specifically:

handicap |handē kap|
noun
a condition that markedly restricts a person's ability to function physically, mentally, or socially.

# MICHAEL J. CARLSON

**Fun facts:**

The American Spinal Injury Association first published an international classification of spinal cord injury in 1982, called the International Standards for Neurological and Functional Classification of Spinal Cord Injury. The latest version, the 6th edition, is still used to document sensory and motor impairments following spinal cord injury. It's based on neurological responses, including light touch and pinprick sensations and strength of 10 key muscles on each side of the body, including hip flexion, shoulder shrug, elbow flexion, wrist extension, and elbow extension.

The symptoms your fictional character may experience after spinal cord injury will vary depending on where the spine is injured and the extent of the injury. Spinal injury can cause your character pain, numbness, or loss of sensation or movement in specific parts of the body, including the skin. An area of the skin innervated by a specific part of the spine is called a dermatome, and a group of muscles innervated by a specific portion of the spine is called a myotome.

A spinal cord injury as used in this context refers to any injury to the spinal cord that is caused by trauma instead of disease. Depending on the section of the spinal cord and nerve roots damaged, the symptoms can vary widely, from pain to paralysis to incontinence. Spinal cord injuries are described as "incomplete," which can vary from having no effect on the character to "complete" which means a total loss of function below that level.

In an incomplete injury, some or all of the functions below the injured area may be unaffected. In a complete spinal injury, all function below the injured, segment is lost. Complete injury frequently means that your patient will have little hope of functional recovery. The relative incidence of incomplete injuries compared to complete spinal cord injury has improved over the past half-century, mainly due to the emphasis on better initial care and stabilization of spinal cord injuries.

The best way to understand the potential implications of spinal cord injury after trauma to your character is a basic understanding of the specific parts of the body that may be affected by paralysis and/or loss of function after an injury. Since the spinal column is conveniently separated into cervical (neck), thoracic (chest), and lumbar (lower back) segments, let's look at them in that order.

A word about standard nomenclature and shorthand: the bones of the cervical spine are referred to with the capital letter "C", the thoracic spine, with the capital letter "T", and the lumbar and sacral portions of the spine use the designations "L" and "S" respectively. The individual vertebrae (plural of vertebra) are designated using numbers, with the 5th cervical vertebra, for instance being referred to as C-5 and the 7th thoracic vertebra T-7, etc. While anatomically, there are 7 cervical vertebrae, 12 thoracic vertebrae, 5 lumbar vertebrae, one sacral bone, when we refer to the nerve roots exiting the spinal cord, they do so in the spaces between the vertebrae.

The cervical spine is unique in that the nerve root that exits between the 7th cervical vertebra and the 1st thoracic vertebra is referred to as the 8th cervical nerve or C-8. However, the nerve root that exits between the 12th thoracic and 1st lumbar vertebrae is referred to as T-12 and the nerve root that exists between the 5th lumbar vertebra and the sacrum, L-5. Hey, I didn't make this stuff up, I just report it.

Also, anatomically, the spinal cord technically stops at T-12. The nerves that continue into the lumbar, sacral, and coccygeal portion of the spine are comprised of nerve roots referred to as the *cauda equina* which is Latin for "horse's tail."

The sacrum of the fetus and children is composed of 5 bones which eventually fuse to form the heart-shaped structure seen at the base of the spine on human skeletons. There are 5 corresponding sacral nerves that exit through small holes on the front side of the sacrum and innervate portions of the pelvis, genitals, legs, and feet.

We have no idea what the coccyx does except to provide one measly coccygeal nerve. The only thing the coccygeal nerve does is hurt when your character slips and falls onto her backside, keeping the makers of inflatable donuts in business. Nature—go figure.

## The cervical spine

Neck injuries usually result in full or partial quadriplegia. However, depending on the specific location, nature, and severity of the injury, your character may retain limited function above the level of injury. If your character is injured at the first or second cervical level, referred to as the C-1/C-2 level, he'll lose the ability to breathe spontaneously, usually resulting in death. If he survives, he'll require either a mechanical ventilator or a surgically implanted phrenic nerve pacemaker. Additionally, cervical injuries at this level typically include the inability or reduced ability to regulate heart rate, blood pressure, sweating and body temperature regulation, and reduces the body's normal responses to pain and/or sensory disturbances below the neck. Sucks, big time.

Please note: problems noted here should be understood to include loss of function below the level indicated as well as at the level indicated. Sensory and motor function above the level of injury should remain relatively unaffected. What this means to your character is that he will retain sensation in and use of his arms if his injury is in the thoracic spine or lower as those nerves exit from the cervical spine.

At the C-3 vertebral level, your character can expect the loss of diaphragm function, requiring the use of a ventilator for breathing. Injury at the C-4 level will result in a significant loss of function of everything below your character's biceps and shoulders. A C-5 level injury will probably result in some mild loss of function at the shoulders and biceps (upper arm muscles), and loss of function at the wrists and hands, and below. Your character can expect limited wrist control and a complete loss of hand function if their injury is at the C6 level, while injury to the C-7 and T-1 nerve roots results in a lack of dexterity in the hands and fingers and below, but does allow limited use of the arms.

A quick note here: The sensory nerves responsible for the sense of touch, temperature, taste, smell, and vibration, and movement of the face and head do not exit from the spinal column, and therefore, will not be directly affected by damage there. The nerves responsible for these functions are called cranial nerves and are part of the central nervous system, as is the spinal cord itself. The cranial nerves exit directly from the brain through tiny holes in the skull, bypassing the spinal column.

### The thoracic spine

The thoracic spine provides innervation to the chest, including the nerves running between the ribs (called, oddly enough, the intercostal nerves—anatomists tend to be somewhat lacking in imagination, fortunately). Complete injuries at or below the thoracic spine levels usually will result in paraplegia for your character. Functions of the hands, arms, neck, and breathing are typically unaffected.

Injuries to the T1 through T8 vertebra can be expected to result in the inability to control the abdominal muscles, affecting trunk stability. The rule of thumb here is, the lower the level of injury in the spine, the less severe will be the effects on your character. Proceeding lower through the thoracic spine, injuries to the T-9 through T-12 levels will probably result in at least partial loss of trunk and abdominal muscle control for your character.

### The Lumbosacral spine

Injuries to the lumbar or sacral regions of the spine generally result in decreased control of the legs and hips, urinary system, and defecation. The sacrum is that heart-shaped bone at the bottom of the spine that sits between your character's pelvic bones. Since bowel and bladder function is regulated by the sacral nerves, bowel and bladder dysfunctions and incontinence are very common after significant traumatic injury.

Sexual function is also associated with the sacral spinal segments, and an injury to this area or above would be expected to have significant effects on your character's ability to perform and enjoy sex.

# MICHAEL J. CARLSON

**Syndromes of incomplete injury**

As if we needed something to make the whole concept of the wiring harness more complex, spinal cord injuries may be incomplete as noted above, resulting in retention of some functions but not others or unusual symptoms such as "central cord syndrome," which is a form of incomplete spinal cord injury also referred to as inverse paraplegia, where the hands and arms are paralyzed while the legs and lower extremities work normally. A milder incomplete injury to the cervical or upper thoracic spinal cord may result in some weakness of the arms with relative sparing of the legs and with variable sensory loss.

Injuries to the anterior spinal cord (anterior equals the front of the body) are often associated with flexion type injuries to the cervical spine. Below the level of injury, motor function, pain, and temperature sensation are lost while light touch, sense of position in space, and sense of vibration remain intact.

Injuries to the posterior spinal cord (posterior equals the back of the body) can also occur but are very rare. Damage to this portion of the spinal cord causes a loss of sense of position in space and stereognosis (the ability to perceive and recognize the form of an object using cues from texture, size, spatial properties, and temperature) below the level of injury, while motor function, pain sensation, and sensitivity to light touch all remain intact. So, as an example, your character with an injury to this portion of the spinal cord can see where her leg or foot is, but can't tell it's position with her eyes closed. Nor will she know she's moving her foot over a round object, like a tennis ball or a rolling pin without looking.

Exercise: sit in any chair, put a pencil on the floor, take one of your shoes off, and run your foot over the pencil. Even with your eyes closed, you can tell what the object is from its shape and how it feels. In this injury, your character will know her foot is touching something, she just won't be able to determine what the something is without looking.

There is also a condition known in medical circles as Brown-Sequard

Syndrome. In this syndrome, injuries due to penetrating wounds (e.g. Gunshot wounds or knife penetrations) can result in a loss of motor function, loss of sense of position in space, loss of vibration and light touch on the same side as the injury while your character would experience a loss of pain, temperature, and crude touch sensations on the other side of the body below the level of the injury.

And now for the good news—The weasel clause as promised
Rarely, a shockwave effect from a gunshot wound or explosion, or swelling or hemorrhaging due to other injuries, including falls, can result in temporary loss of function in the spinal cord. If this is the case, your character will probably experience loss of function below the level of injury that will improve or resolve over time as healing takes place. They may have to relearn how to use their extremities again after such an injury, but given enough time and persistence, they may regain nearly everything they originally lost.

Regarding that healing/relearning process: Learning how to walk again as an adult is not the same as learning how to walk the first time. As children, when we learned to walk the first time, we essentially "stumbled" into it. Relearning how to walk will typically be a long, involved, painful process for your character, whether it be from the temporary spinal cord injury, a significant head trauma, or after reawakening from an extended coma. There are, for instance, approximately seventy-five separate commands necessary to take a single step that your character will need to relearn.

# SIX

## STRANGULATION

grabbing the reader by the throat

*"Strangling is the most intimate way to kill someone."*

— Lauren Kate, *Rapture*

**A note to the reader—this section contains information that may be somewhat disturbing to some. Please be aware that strangulation may have significant emotional impact for your reader. For this reason, strangulation may be used in many forms of fiction and in many circumstances, especially if the author decides to "push the edge of the envelope" with regards to readers' emotions. Use carefully, your mileage may vary.

Strangulation is defined as blocking the flow of oxygen to the brain by compression of the neck with the goal of unconsciousness or death. Strangling does not have to be fatal. The state of decreased oxygenation to the brain and the damage it causes can be limited, as in erotic asphyxia or the choking game (fainting game), and is an important technique in combat training and many self-defense systems. Strangulation has been used in literature as long as there has been literature.

Strangulation can be conveniently divided into three types, according to the mechanism.

### Hanging
In this context, hanging is suspension of the character from a rope, cord, or some other flexible device wound around the neck, using the body's own

weight to compress the neck, usually resulting in unconsciousness in a few seconds, followed by death. Hanging can be as simple as tying a braided length of bed sheet to some convenient plumbing and partially suspending the victim (as is often the case in prison suicides) or as complex as judicial hangings, which are often very elaborate. Used traditionally in capital punishment, there are very few countries left that employ judicial hanging.

In the case where judicial hanging is used as a plot device (as in the staged execution of Moist von Lipwig in *Going Postal* by Terry Pratchett), the writer should be aware that unconsciousness is almost instantaneous followed by death within minutes unless the hangman is very careful and exceedingly good with details.

## Ligature strangulation

Is strangulation by a cord around the neck (called a garrote) like hanging, but without suspension of the body. Ligature strangulation is used historically as a form of murder (suicide by ligature being somewhat impractical). This method of strangulation is often practiced in combat arenas where stealth is necessary, and against an opponent who is larger and/or stronger than the aggressor. It was used extensively during the Spanish inquisition against victims who admitted their alleged sins and recanted. It gained a certain prominence in the twentieth century as a popular means of murder employed by the American Mafia and illustrated in the movie *The Godfather*. It's used extensively in spy novels, war novels, and action/mystery novels, although not commonly from the point of view of the victim (as they usually die as a result, effectively eliminating them as a main character).

## Manual strangulation

Involves strangulation using the fingers or another extremity (i.e. the inner surface of the elbow is commonly used in chokeholds). Blunt objects, such as batons are also used in this method.

Historically, manual strangulation, also known as "throttling," is sometimes used in "crimes of passion." It's most commonly in men against women, children, or the elderly and not in man against man, as it generally requires a significant inequality in strength between the aggressor and the victim. Mary Shelly employed this method extensively in Frankenstein, giving the monster free reign to do away with much of Victor's family in this manner as revenge for bringing him to life.

Some properly executed choke holds, however, are normally accomplished from behind, require less physical strength, and can be performed by smaller persons against larger victims.

Unconsciousness and/or death are a result of either partially or completely blocking the flow of oxygen to the brain (hypoxia). This is accomplished by either blocking blood flow at the carotid arteries as they are the primary carriers of blood to the brain or by blocking air flow by compressing the airway, thereby preventing oxygen entering the lungs. It's fairly easy to compress the carotid arteries, as the estimated force required to compress them is ~3.4 N/cm2 or about 5-6 pounds per square inch, in the countries using the English measure. The trachea (airway) in the neck is a bit more difficult to compress, due to bands of cartilage almost completely encircling it. It's kind of like crushing a vacuum cleaner hose with your bare hands. The estimated force required to compress the trachea is ~22 N/cm2 or in the neighborhood of 30-35 pounds per square inch or roughly 6-7 times the force required for the carotid arteries.

To put these numbers into context, the average 25-year-old man can generate in the neighborhood of 121 pounds per square inch in the dominant hand, and 110 pounds per square inch on the non-dominant side. The ladies are a little daintier, coming in at 70 and 61 pounds per square inch, respectively. Plenty strong enough to do the deed, though. Age does have a bearing. The average 75-year-old male can still get a job with the Corleone Family, at 65 and 55 PSI, and the ladies hang in well, so to speak, still able to generate 42 and 37 PSI at 75 years of age. So, to put that into perspective, your average grandmother can still throttle your average grandfather in his sleep. Maybe all you guys should think twice before leaving the toilet seat up again.

# HURTING YOUR CHARACTERS

## Chokeholds

Are used to cut off blood flow to the brain. Properly applied, this is a safer and more reliable way for one character to render another unconscious than whacking him/her on the head. However, it does carry an inherent risk of causing a stroke, brain damage, or death if the choked character doesn't regain consciousness fairly quickly, usually within a few seconds to a few minutes.

The idea here is that your character is being rendered unconscious because there is so little oxygen getting to the brain that it cannot remain awake. When the police or judo practitioners utilize this move (it was allowed in judo tournaments for years), occasionally, the victim will die. In the case of the police, this usually makes headlines. Strangulation is not anesthesia, as much as Hollywood likes to portray it as such. During general anesthesia, a patient is given drugs to render them unconscious and oxygen to keep them alive, and they are watched by experts, and sometimes they still die.

In literature, television, and in movies, considerable artistic license is taken and murder by suffocation is almost universally quick and easy. One character holds a pillow over the face of another, and the victim will struggle for ten seconds or so, and simply die. A pillow over a character's face has become a subliminal cue that the character is already dead, and once dead, they will be dead for real, with no chance for revival. While there is some justification for this, (most people who are killed in this manner are weakened, sick, or otherwise infirm), a pillow is actually quite porous, allowing small amounts of air to pass through. So even if a pillow is pressed against a victim's face as tightly as possible, it will be a slower, more painful death than other ways of depriving the victim of air.

Attempted murder by strangulation is similar, although the person being strangled is more likely to survive, often with the aggressor suddenly "coming to his/her senses" at the last possible moment (usually referred to as "the what have I done moment") stopping just short of finishing their victim off.

So, what happens to your character during strangulation?

In all forms of strangulation, the initial response is an immediate and profound air hunger and panic, initially causing the heart rate to increase. If pressure is applied to the carotid arteries, small pressure sensors contained within them are stimulated, resulting in a sudden heart rate reduction by as much as 30%. Your character's vision will blur and tunnel, going dark around the edges. Your character's mouth, fingers, and toes will start to tingle and they may have a sensation of euphoria. As the asphyxiation deepens, your character's heart rate will slow and they will begin to weaken, their muscles going slack as unconsciousness pushes in. Finally, the scene in front of them will telescope away to a pinpoint, and disappear as they lose consciousness. Death occurs a few minutes later.

Unconsciousness generally occurs between 10 seconds and one minute, depending on the effectiveness of the technique applied, with death occurring within a few minutes. Before you breathe a sigh of relief over those numbers, it can be a long 10 seconds, especially if your character's adversary is fighting back. An excellent portrayal of a strangulation murder was demonstrated in the third episode of the first season of the series *Breaking Bad*. The main character (Walter) is forced to strangle a drug dealer with a steel bicycle lock while he's stabbed in the leg repeatedly with a shard of broken dinner plate, and it's one of the longest 40 seconds in television.

**Drowning**
Drowning is, likewise, quicker in the media that in reality, but a character in the water will typically thrash and splash in an extended struggle for several long minutes. This is usually accompanied by repeated, unanswered shouts for help, often slipping under the surface several times, but each time, a fear-driven adrenaline surge will propel the character to the surface until, at last, exhausted, all hope gone, she goes down for the last time. She may even utter a few last words before succumbing. If brought to shore quickly, the character can usually be resuscitated, unless the victim is the main victim of a murder mystery or thriller. In those instances, the victim of foul play cannot be revived, even after having been submerged in cold water for a few minutes, unlike real life, where a lowered body temperature sometimes shunts oxygen-

rich blood away from the extremities, allowing resuscitation even after tens of minutes of submersion. In fact, if the water is cold, it's considered a positive sign. Controlled hypothermia after successful cardiac resuscitation is currently being taught, as it's been found to aid in preserving brain cells during the critical period.

In reality, while a person may make a scene before they start to drown, often a person who is drowning will gradually weaken, eventually flapping their arms against the water to no effect, trying to push their mouth above water. An untrained observer may not even realize that the swimmer is in trouble until it's too late. Professional lifeguards are trained to observe for telltale signs that a swimmer is unable to keep their mouth above the surface or fail to respond to spoken commands. Children, in particular, are noisy in the water. A quiet child in the water is usually cause for alarm. This is especially true for toddlers, who still possess a strong diving reflex. Young children who fall into a pool will often simply stop breathing and sink to the bottom.

A tangent here about the mammalian diving reflex. The mammalian diving reflex is a response in mammals, of which we are one branch, which optimizes respiration to allow submersion in the water for extended periods. It's exhibited strongly in other, aquatic mammals, like seals, otters, dolphins, etc., but exists in other members (e.g. us) and in diving birds, such as penguins, to a smaller degree. The diving reflex is triggered specifically by cold water contacting the face. Immersion in water warmer than 21 °C (70 °F) often doesn't initiate the response, nor does submersion of other body parts. The reflex is stronger in children and is one reason they tend to be more responsive to resuscitation after drowning than adults.

So what will you character experience in drowning or near-drowning? Her heart rate will slow between ten and twenty-five percent, as part of the dive reflex noted above. The slowed heart rate reduces the heart's demand for oxygen, leaving more for the brain. Next, capillaries (the small blood vessels) in the skin and the arms and legs close, restricting flow to those areas, beginning with the fingers and toes, proceeding to the hands and feet, extending to the arms and legs, eventually stopping blood flow to all the extremities. Unlike aquatic mammals who can store 25-30% of their oxygen storage in muscle, humans only store about 12% of the body's total oxygen in the muscles, so cramping begins in this phase. Sensation from these areas will also diminish, leaving them numb. Then blood flow to the "nonessential" organs in the abdomen is shunted away, retaining oxygen flow to the brain and heart.

The last phase of the reflex only occurs in very deep dives. The blood vessel walls allow plasma to flow freely into the chest cavity, keeping the pressure constant so the lungs aren't crushed. The plasma filling the *alveoli*, the tiny bunches of air sacks where gas exchange takes place, is reabsorbed when the animal leaves the pressurized environment. This reaction has been observed in world-class freedivers. If your character reaches this level, there will be almost no unusual sensations from the chest, as the majority of nerve impulses from organs like the lungs has to do with pressure changes and the point of the lungs filling with fluid is to keep the pressure equalized.

Examples of the mammalian diving reflex in literature and film include *Starfish*, by Peter Watts, and the films *The Abyss* by James Cameron, and *Die Another Day* by Neal Purvis and Robert Wade.
http://en.wikipedia.org/wiki/Mammalian_diving_reflex

## Incomplete strangulation

In incomplete strangulation, reduced oxygenation leads to a buildup of carbon dioxide (one of the body's waste products), which causes the muscle spasms, tingling and numbness in the fingers and toes and around the mouth, dizziness, and a sense of giddiness or euphoria. This is where erotic asphyxia enters the picture. Erotic asphyxia is the enhancement of sexual arousal by accompanied asphyxia. There has been recent research that suggests an abnormality in neurotransmitters increases an individual's predisposition toward erotic asphyxia (referred to as 'gaspers' in slang terminology, and often as 'the deceased' in official circles). For a very small segment of the population, the combination of orgasm and asphyxiation is as powerful and addicting as cocaine use. Word of warning—DO NOT TRY THIS AT HOME or at a hotel.

# HURTING YOUR CHARACTERS

This sense of euphoria is the basis of the somewhat more benign fainting game (also know as the choking game and by a wide variety of local slang terms—see below), or self-induced hypoxia. This practice, almost always involving children or adolescents, is distinctly different from erotic asphyxiation, which is oxygen deprivation combined with sexual arousal.

Limited research has been done into motivations for the fainting game, but it appears to be pursued exclusively by children and adolescents as a way of "thrill-seeking" with the perception of low-risk. From the studies done, estimates range from 10 to 20 percent of youths aged 12-18 years reported practicing the fainting game at some time.

Other names include: The Fainting Game, Riding a Rocket, Airplaning, America Dream Game, Black Out Game, Breath Play, Bum Rushing, California Choke, California Dreaming, California Headrush, California High, California Knockout, Choking Out, Cloud Nine, Dumbass Game, Dying game, Dream Game, Dreaming Game, Elevator, Flatline Game, Flat Liner, Flatliner Game, Funky Chicken, Harvey Wallbanger, Hyperventilation Game, Indian Headrush, Knockout Game, Pass-out Game, Passing Out Game, Natural High, Sleeper Hold, Space Cowboy, Space Monkey, Suffocation Game, Suffocation Roulette, Teen Choking Game, Rising Sun, High Riser, Tingling Game, Trip to Heaven, Rocket Ride and Speed Dreaming, Wall-Hit, Purple Dragon, and Five second high. I have no idea why California plays such a frequent role in the slang, and not, say, New Jersey or Kansas.

Recovery times vary after incomplete strangulation and drowning depending on the length of time and the degree to which the brain is deprived of oxygen. Hollywood would have us believe that a strangled character dies as soon as they lose consciousness. Like most things Hollywood, though, this is not an accurate representation of the process. In reality, death occurs several minutes after unconsciousness, and only then if the oxygen deprivation to the brain is continued. If blood flow returns, the character will awaken in a few seconds to a few minutes, usually with a considerable headache from the carbon dioxide buildup and sore throat from local tissue bruising. It would normally take several minutes for the character to regain enough strength to stand without assistance and a couple of hours before she felt strong enough for extensive physical activity. It would also be expected that a young, otherwise healthy character could recover completely in a few days. A possible exception to this would be due to damage to the larynx (vocal cords). This would be likely in cases of hanging, garroting, and manual strangulation, and might cause sore or scratchy throat and vocal hoarseness for a few days to a few weeks and possibly permanent voice changes.

**To the reader:**

Again, I'm mindful of the emotional nature this particular topic and the effect its discussion may have on the reader. I apologize once more for any discomfort it may cause. That is not my intent. I've made every effort to remain somewhat clinical when writing this chapter, and for that reason, it may read somewhat flatter than other chapters.

# SEVEN

## LACERATIONS & INCISIONS

*"Tears sprang from her eyes and she bit her lip to stop herself from howling at the bright pain."*

— Stephen M. Irwin, *The Dead Path*

**Lacerations**

A laceration is defined as a tearing of the skin, usually leaving a somewhat rough, jagged edge, usually with some degree of bruising at the edges. A cut, on the other hand, is more properly described as an incision, where the edges are sharp and clean. Incisions also typically bleed more than lacerations, as the blood vessels are more cleanly divided.

Often, the two terms are used interchangeably in literature and the movies, so we'll bow to convention this time and refer to both as cuts, with the understanding that we're talking about a traumatic event with the intent to do your character harm and not an intentional surgical procedure. Besides, laceration has a lot more letters, and I have to type this. Things one character can use to cut another are almost as varied as the characters' personalities. Usually, a metal implement of some sort, but writers can be very inventive when it comes to edged weapons, and I've read stories and seen movies where materials as diverse as glass, pottery, wood, stone, ice, and plastic have found uses in the fertile imaginations of writers.

In the end, almost any hard, sharp material will suffice in a pinch.

**Mechanism of injury**

In general, there are 4 types of lacerations:

Split laceration. This type of wound occurs when a body part is crushed between 2 objects, but not as seriously as in a crush injury. Blunt force is applied on areas where the skin is in close proximity to bone and subcutaneous tissues are scanty. A split laceration may produce a wound which looks like an incised wound. Typical sites for these wounds are scalp, eyebrows, cheekbones, lower jaw, iliac crest, and perineum (that one's not nearly as funny as it sounds at first).

Stretch laceration. This kind of injury is typically caused by a single, angular force that strikes and either pushes or pulls the skin, causing it to stretch and break. An example of an over-stretching wound is a gunshot. The bullet presses on the skin, compressing and stretching it as it continues on, until at some point the forces exhibited overwhelm the tensile strength of the skin, causing it to rip and tear. Because bullets are not sharp objects, they technically do not pierce the skin as much as tear their way through, leaving a hole with a ragged edge. Also commonly seen when a character is run over by a motor vehicle, tearing the skin until it produces a flap.

Tension laceration (Avulsion—see below). When an object strikes the skin with a blunt impact at either an angle or with a sweeping motion, the resulting laceration is considered a tension laceration. This injury occurs in much the same manner as peeling a potato, when the object strikes the skin, the tissue is crushed beneath the epidermis and the top layer of the skin simply peels away.

Tear laceration. Probably the most common kind of laceration. This kind of injury can result in either a clean sharp, incisional edge at one extreme or a ragged, torn-appearing edge at the other, usually depending on how sharp the implement is. Usually occurs from impacts against irregular or sharp objects, like the handle of a car door (one of the reasons car door handles are made the way they are, now).

# HURTING YOUR CHARACTERS

Getting cut open is firmly in the Not Nice Column and most human beings come equipped with a healthy set of defensive reflexes to avoid it. If at all possible they will try to put something else (like hands or arms) in the way of an attack. Most people injured by an edged weapon have injuries on their upper extremities as well from trying to ward off their assailant, called "defensive wounds" by professionals.

As we discussed briefly in Chapter 2, the severity of a cut depends a great deal on its location and depth. The degree to which a cut hurts is dependent to a large degree on the length of the cut and how jagged the edges are. That makes sense if you think about it for a minute. The reason a cut hurts is because the nerve endings in the skin are suddenly exposed to the air, which causes a rapid pH change due to the drying effect of air. The more nerves are damaged and exposed to the air, the worse the cut hurts, typically. There are occasional exceptions to this rule of thumb, but it will mostly get you where you want to take your characters, which is into danger and suffering.

Side note: blood smells like _____. Blood is described in many ways by many people. Fresh blood is most often noted to have a subtle "metallic" scent, while old, dried blood is usually described as a combination of a penny in your mouth and rotting meat. Ick (oops, author intrusion).

## Limbs

The arms and legs are not protected by much flesh so even a shallow cut may damage bone and muscle and render the limb effectively useless. Another consideration is that severe blood loss can occur if the major blood vessels in the inside of the upper arm and inner thigh are damaged. There are some fairly large blood vessels in the extremities, raising the possibility that your character may lose enough blood to render her unconscious or worse (more about blood loss in chapter 8). That having been said, there are very few vital organs located in the extremities, so they are better suited to taking the brunt of an attack and being used in self-defense.

While cuts generally hurt, the injury to your character may involve nerve damage. In this case, your character will experience some degree of numbness or loss of movement in the extremity distal to (on the far side of) the injury. This is because the nerve has been severed.

In the good news column, peripheral nerves do have limited ability to regenerate, allowing your character the potential to eventually regain sensation and use of the extremity. A side note here; in a young, otherwise healthy adult, peripheral nerves regenerate at approximately 1 mm per day from the injury site to the end of the extremity. This regeneration rate is the same for either sex. So, the idea here is if your character receives a laceration, let's say on the arm, and they notice numbness extending from the injury all the way to the fingers, the distance from the injury to the tips of the affected fingers, measured in millimeters, represents the number of days it will probably take for that nerve to regain sensation. Sometimes, permanent residual numbness remains even after the character experiences some the nerve regeneration, which the character will be aware of while not be noticeable to other characters. This is especially useful in cases where the character or the back story needs a permanent reminder of some traumatic incident from that character's past.

## Abdomen

Lacerations in the abdomen will bleed a lot and can easily do fatal damage to your character, but unless a main artery is hit it's not going to be a quick death. Anything more than 2 inches deep starts to get dangerous. An important consideration here would be a highly vascular organ such as the liver. If your character sustains a significant injury to the right side of the abdomen, just under the ribs, they have a better chance of dying through hemorrhage (rapid blood loss) because of the amount of blood passing through the liver.

Injury to the abdominal organs can be expected to cause bleeding, infections and a nasty slow death for your character if left untreated. Bleeding from the spleen or liver can cause death in as little as 20 minutes. Less major damage to internal organs would cause death either from blood loss over several hours or up to several days later from infection and other complications.

Relatively minor cuts to the stomach area could damage muscles and affect breathing.

Major cuts to the abdomen can damage nerves and muscles, meaning the injured character would have no control over their legs. Not nice when you're trying to get away from the wingnut who's just sliced you up and suddenly your legs don't work…

Extensive cuts here can also mean the insides are suddenly outside, known in technical terms as evisceration. Not pretty, not comfortable and, untreated, leaves the character with about 15 minutes to live while they're going into shock, and they're going to wish it was much less. Quite apart from the pain (which is pretty horrific) the sight of their own insides tends to make most people quite hysterical. And, if that weren't bad enough, if the cut is extensive enough, opening the intestine, your character will have the added embarrassment of that awful smell of yesterday's lunch being suddenly on the sidewalk.

## Chest

Lacerations to the chest tend to be fairly superficial because of all those handy ribs standing between the blade and the important parts. However, because of the nature of lacerations (usually involving things like blunt trauma), there could be underlying damage to those ribs which could, in turn, result in damage to important organs like the lungs or heart. This is covered more effectively in chapter 9 and Chapter 10.

## Subjective symptoms

So, then, what will your character feel when he's cut? Initially, depending on the sharpness of the blade, maybe not much. Probably, though, your character will experience a sudden, sharp, searing, intense, excruciating pain as the edge slices through the skin. This is known as "first pain." After the initial insult, the sharp, intense pain will start to subside, and the site will start to throb, burn, and ache, becoming more of a dull pain. This is referred to as "second pain" and can go on for hours to days, depending on the severity of the injury and whether the character receives care or not.

Muscles and internal organs don't transmit pain signals the same way as the skin (please refer beck to that incredibly boring chapter 2). Organs generally only sense tension. But wait, you say, what about pressure, like that of having to really, really urinate (can I say "urinate" here?). Yeah, I think I can. Anyway, your character really has to go, and she's squirming in her seat, sweat beading on her forehead, with pressure rapidly building in her bladder. What she's actually feeling as her bladder expands to what feels like the size of a beach ball, is the tension, pulling in every direction, much like filling a balloon with water. And that sensation can be very painful, progressing from a faint, uncomfortable "full" feeling, through the dull ache stage, finally landing in you character's lap as a severe, cramping, burning pressure that brings tears to her eyes until… oops, never mind.

Slicing with a sharp blade is a different story. He'll usually feel a sting, then it only hurts when air gets into the cut initially. If the skin closes up on its own you get a dull ache after a while that can increase depending on depth. The closure is not perfect then it burns much like a severe paper cut.

### Abrasion/avulsion

The minor injuries side of abrasion is covered in Chapter 2. This chapter discusses grade 2 and higher avulsion injuries.

Second-degree abrasions typically involve the dermis as well as the epidermis and may bleed significantly. This level of injury to your character can be compared to a second-degree burn after the blister has broken leaving exposed deeper layers of skin. The area will be very tender for your character for a few days as healing starts, also similar to a second-degree burn.

Third-degree abrasions involve damage to the subcutaneous layer of skin and are often called avulsions. Avulsions are much more serious an injury for your character (the word avulsion comes from the Latin word avullere, or "to tear off"). Most commonly the term third-degree avulsion refers to the surface injury where all the layers of skin have been torn away, exposing the underlying structures (e.g. Subcutaneous fat, muscle, and tendon). However, other body parts may be detached at the same time.

# HURTING YOUR CHARACTERS

### Ear and eye avulsions

I've included ear and eyelid avulsions in with the more serious injuries because, although these injuries are not necessarily life-threatening, they will certainly stop your character in their tracks.

### Ear avulsions

Ears are particularly vulnerable to avulsion injuries because of their exposed position. Ears can be partially or completely avulsed and may be reattached using microvascular surgery. There's usually a higher success rate for partially avulsed ears. The most common mechanism of injury in ear avulsions is human bites, followed by falls, motor vehicle crashes, and dog bites.

### Eyelid avulsions

Eyelid avulsions are uncommon. The most common mechanism of these injuries are motor vehicle accidents, dog bites, and human bites. Reconstruction is usually possible with variable degrees of success. Because of the extraordinarily high numbers of sensory nerves per square millimeter located on the face and ears, this type of injury would typically be expected to result in considerable sharp, searing, throbbing pain for the character. The phrase "keep an eye peeled" takes on a whole new meaning. So... when one peels an eye, does it come off in thin onion-like layers or like an orange?

### Brachial plexus avulsions

In a brachial plexus avulsion, the nerve bundle that sends impulses from the spine to the arms, shoulders, and hands is torn from its attachment to the spine. A common cause of this injury is shoulder rotation of the baby in the birth canal during delivery, although adults sometimes experience the same injury for other reasons (motor vehicle crashes and athletic injuries, like football, wrestling, and cage fighting are common sources of injury). Detachment of the nerve bundle causes severe pain and loss of function in the affected arm. Occasionally, the nerve bundle can be reattached.

### Degloving injuries

A degloving injury is a type of avulsion in which an extensive section of skin is

78

completely torn off the underlying tissue (usually of an extremity), completely severing its blood supply. The name comes from the analogy of removing a glove. An example of this kind of injury in film is in the Terminator 2 (Judgment Day) film where the T-100 removes the skin of its own hand to prove to Miles Dyson that it's a machine. A degloving injury can involve a finger (usually the left ring finger, a hand, toe(s), or even scalp or face. Farm machinery and some manufacturing processes (like printing presses) were historically notorious for this type of injury, but in the case of a facial degloving injury, animal attacks are the more common cause.

This injury commonly happens extraordinarily quickly (because of the usual mechanism being associated with, well, mechanisms). The result is the person sometimes feels a firm tug in the extremity, pulls back from reflex, and looks down to see part of the skin covering their hand or foot is gone. That's when the pain usually starts. Injuries of this nature can be surgically repaired if the skin can be recovered. Otherwise, the only options are skin grafting, scar formation, or amputation of the affected part. In any of the three, the rehabilitation process is long, involved, and painful. Your hero won't be grappling with any crooks anytime soon.

### Incised wounds

An incised wound is a clean cut through the tissues, which is (usually) longer than it is deep. This type of wound is produced by the pressure and friction against the tissue by an object having a sharp cutting edge, e.g., a knife, razor, scalpel, etc.

The edges of an incised wound are typically clean cut, well-defined, and usually free from contusions. Incisions typically bleed more than lacerations because blood vessels are cut cleanly. Incised wounds are normally deeper at the beginning of the incision because that is where the greatest pressure is. This is known as the "head of the wound." The incision becomes increasingly shallow toward the end of the cut, finally, only the skin is cut. This is known as the "tail of the wound."

A subset of incised wounds is chop wounds. These wounds are caused by a blow with a sharp cutting edge of a fairly heavy instrument like an ax, butcher's cleaver, machete, etc. The dimensions of the wound roughly correspond to the cross-section of penetrating blade. These injuries can also damage the underlying bone, with symptoms similar to fractures (Chapter 10).

# EIGHT

## PENETRATING TRAUMA

*"The best armor is to keep out of gunshot."*

—Francis Bacon

**Penetrating trauma**

Many if not all of popular literature's action-adventure series heroes have been shot and/or stabbed at least once in those series. Janet Evanovich's Stephanie Plum and Sue Grafton's Kinsey Millhone come immediately to mind, as does Lee Child's Jack Reacher character with varying results (Stephanie Plum was shot twice, Kinsey Millhone once, and Jack Reacher at least once).

Penetrating injuries are the result of an object entering the body and sometimes exiting the body and causing damage along the path (trajectory). Occasionally, the object remains in the body, becoming a foreign object. A general rule for this type of injury is that any wound deeper than it is wide is, by definition, a penetrating wound. The size of the object, its speed, direction, point of entry, energy transfer, and the path the object takes are important considerations for your character when injuring them in this manner.

Because of the mechanism of injury in penetrating wounds, the damage it does to the character is often out of proportion to the size of the entry wound. For this reason, penetrating wounds are generally broken down into three categories; low energy, medium energy, and high energy wounds. A low energy wound is any wound that is delivered using the strength of a human and usually only does damage to the area of contact. Examples of low energy wounds your character is likely to encounter are; knives, ice picks, spears, and even arrows.

Arrows are considered a low energy wound because even though the arrow is delivered from a bow and often at considerably higher speed than is possible with an arm alone, the bow is still drawn and the arrow is still held using one's own strength. This is different from a crossbow, which is either drawn by hand or cranked into tension using a ratcheted mechanism, and held in tension by another mechanism, which then releases the bolt. Dropping into a punji pit would probably be considered a low energy injury. Nasty, but low energy. Gravity, in general, is considered in a later chapter.
https://en.wikipedia.org/wiki/Penetrating_trauma

Medium energy wounds are delivered by things like crossbows, handguns, or shotguns, and machine guns. Because the kinetic energy increases roughly at the square of the velocity (that pesky physics thing again), the amount of damage done to the underlying structures is much higher in the case of medium energy wounds than that of low energy wounds. Personally, I have trouble imaging what a low-powered rifle would look like or be used for. Maybe a blunderbuss, but really?

High energy penetrating wounds are formed by higher mass/higher velocity projectiles, such as high powered rifles. Rifles chambered for 7.62x39 (AK-47 or SKS), or .223/NATO 5.56 (AR-15), 30.06, .308, and 300 Win Mag have muzzle velocities roughly 2-3 times those of handguns. There's a little overlap here, as the fastest handgun (Mag-Safe 9x19 Stealth+P @ 1950 fps) round is slightly higher than the slowest rifle muzzle velocity (.38-40 Win @ 1160 fps).
http://chuckhawks.com/rifle_ballistics_table.htm
http://www.chuckhawks.com/handgun_power_chart.htm

Blast injuries would most likely also fall into the high energy category. Interestingly, a search of the Internet (where all things informational reside these days) reveals there is no exact consensus about what constitutes an assault rifle.

With a low energy wound, your character will probably experience sharp, intense, or even cutting or searing pain depending on the size and shape of the injury. Oddly enough, bullet wounds are often not immediately felt by the victim. Unfortunately, "Hollywood Recoil" where a character is thrown across the room and into a wall by the impact of a bullet is a myth. It would be pretty cool if it worked that way, but it really doesn't. The only realistic example of that kind of reaction would come about by being hit from close range by a shotgun blast and that would mostly just knock your character off his feet and not across the room. Some of the most accurate depictions of the effect of gunshot wounds come in the first five minutes of Saving Private Ryan. Gruesome and difficult to watch, but fairly accurate.

When your character is stabbed, the blade will probably enter and then usually be withdrawn. The initial sensation depends a lot on the speed of the assault. A slow penetration is almost always more painful, as your character will have time to register the the fact that she's been stabbed. A fast jab, on the other hand, will probably hurt a little less at first, with the pain increasing after a few seconds to a minute or two.

The pain swiftly fades to an ache when no major nerves are involved. If there is nerve involvement, your character will not only experience pain at the site because of the initial injury, but she may lose sensation distal to the injury (distal to means in a direction away from the center of the body, so if the injury is to the thigh and a major nerve is damaged, large portions of the leg toward the foot will go numb.

Also, as with lacerations, a thin, sharp knife will leave your character in less pain than dull blade or a sharpened arrowhead.

Bullets. The space left in tissue by the penetrating object as it passes through forms a cavity (the "bullet hole"). This hole is called a permanent cavitation. In addition to causing damage to the tissues they contact, medium and high-velocity projectiles cause a secondary cavitation injury. As the bullet enters the body, it creates a pressure wave which forces tissue out of the way, creating a "temporary cavity" that can be much larger than the bullet itself or the permanent cavity. Because the body is made of pretty elastic stuff (think of it as a bag of Jell-O where bullets are concerned), as the pressure wave dissipates, the tissues then move back into place, eliminating the temporary cavity, but the pressure wave frequently does considerable damage. Temporary cavitation can be especially damaging when it affects delicate organs such as the brain as occurs in penetrating head trauma. This is why exit wounds are almost invariably much larger and messier than entrance wounds.

So, what will your character feel from a gunshot wound? Initially, maybe a quick "snap," like a large rubber band, or a firm slap when the bullet enters, but not necessarily. Within a few seconds, an intense, "white-hot" burning sensation will develop. The shock wave we mentioned above will cause at least temporary paralysis of any extremity with this type of injury. Depending on what the bullet encounters when it gets past the skin (bones, for instance) there may be a solid "thunk" sort of sensation. If a bone is involved, it will almost always fracture, the pressure wave usually shattering the bone right around the path (more about that below). The fracture will provide a severe, deep, burning, dull, poorly localized ache after the initial sharp electric crack from the break.

Okay, so why does being shot hurt so darn much afterward? Prepare yourself, this will be more than you ever wanted to know about being shot (as if you wanted to anything about being shot). There will also be a little more of that darned physics stuff, but as little as possible, I promise, and only then to help explain.

## WOUNDING EFFECTS

### Physical

Permanent and temporary cavitation will cause your character very different biological effects. The effects of a permanent cavity are fairly obvious. A hole through the heart will cause loss of pumping efficiency, loss of blood, and eventually cardiac arrest. A hole through the liver or lung will be similar, with the lung shot having the added effect of reducing blood oxygenation and possibly collapsing due to air leaking out the hole; these effects, however, are generally slower to arise than damage to the heart. A hole through the brain can cause instant unconsciousness and will likely kill your character immediately (but not always). A hole through the spinal cord will instantly interrupt the nerve signals to and from some or all his extremities, disabling your character and in many cases also resulting in death (as the nerve signals to and from the heart and/or lungs are interrupted by a shot high in the chest or to the neck). By contrast, a gunshot wound to an arm or leg which hits only muscle can cause a great deal of pain but is unlikely to be fatal, unless one of the large blood vessels (femoral or brachial arteries, for example) is also severed in the process.

The effects of temporary cavitation are less well understood, due to a lack of a test material identical to living tissue. Studies on the effects of bullets typically are based on experiments using ballistic gelatin, in which temporary cavitation causes radial tears where the gelatin was stretched. Although such tears are visually engaging, some animal tissues (other than bone or liver) are more elastic than gelatin. In most cases, temporary cavitation is likely to cause significant localized bruising. Nerve bundles can be damaged by temporary cavitation, creating a stun effect, but this hasn't been confirmed.

One exception to this is when a very powerful temporary cavity intersects with the spine. In this case, the resulting blunt trauma can slam the vertebrae together hard enough to either sever the spinal cord, or damage it enough to knock out, stun, or paralyze the target. For instance, in the shootout between eight FBI agents and two bank robbers on April 11, 1986, in Miami, Florida, Special Agent Gordon McNeill was struck in the neck by a high-velocity .223 bullet fired by Michael Platt. While the bullet did not directly contact the spine, and the wound incurred wasn't ultimately fatal, the temporary cavitation was sufficient to render SA McNeill paralyzed for several hours. I'd guess that was a pretty emotional few hours for SA McNeill and his loved ones.

Temporary cavitation can also cause tearing of tissue if a very large amount of force is involved, as in very high-velocity rifle bullets or shrapnel. Even at typical handgun velocities, bullets will still create temporary cavities and are capable of causing damage to elastic tissue which they don't directly contact.

Core-locked rifle bullets that strike a major bone (such as a femur) can expend their entire energy into the surrounding tissue, causing it to take on a gelled consistency as the cellular structure is destroyed. The struck bone is commonly shattered at the point of impact (resembling "rice crispies" on an X-ray). These shattered bones are salvageable only through extensive surgeries and long and painful rehabilitation, if at all.

High-velocity fragmentation can also increase the effect of temporary cavitation. The fragments sheared from the bullet cause many small permanent cavities around the main entry point. The main mass of the bullet can then cause a truly massive amount of tearing as the perforated tissue is stretched. This will usually leave your character in severe pain, with fairly rapid blood loss, unable to move the extremity, and rapidly going into shock.

So, why does it hurt to be shot? To summarize, some of the pain is because of the bullet's path through the body (the permanent cavity) because the bullet compresses and rips the body parts it passes through, but the temporary cavity caused by the shock wave of the bullet's path is responsible for more of the surrounding bruising and damage, as it expands and relaxes. This is damage without destruction.

Whether a person or animal will be incapacitated (i.e. "Stopped") when shot depends on a large number of factors including physical, physiological, and psychological effects.

**Psychological**
Emotional shock, terror, or surprise can cause your character to faint, surrender, or flee when shot or shot at. Emotional fainting is the likely reason for most "one-shot stops," and not an intrinsic effectiveness quality of any firearm or bullet. There are many documented instances where people have instantly dropped unconscious when the bullet only hit an extremity or even completely missed. Additionally, the muzzle blast and flash from many

firearms are substantial and can cause disorientation, dazzling, and stunning effects. Flashbangs (stun grenades) and other less-lethal "distraction devices" rely exclusively on these effects.

Pain is another psychological factor and can be enough to dissuade a person from continuing their actions.

Temporary cavitation can emphasize the impact of a bullet since the resulting tissue compression is identical to simple blunt force trauma. It's easier for someone to feel when they've been shot if there's considerable temporary cavitation, and this can contribute to either psychological or physiological factor of incapacitation.

However, if a person is sufficiently enraged, determined, or intoxicated, they can simply shrug off the psychological effects of being shot. Therefore, such effects are not as reliable as physiological effects at stopping people. Animals will not faint or surrender if injured, though they may become frightened by the loud noise and pain of being shot, so psychological mechanisms are generally less effective against non-humans.

This would also be a good time to note that there is no safe place in the body to be shot. A gunshot wound to the leg or shoulder can cause serious bleeding, nerve damage, and death because there are some honkin' big nerves and arteries entering the arms and legs. Penetrating wounds typically take weeks to months to heal depending on the underlying damage and the biggest risk usually infection. Foreign bodies left in the victim almost always become infected.

If the main descending aorta is hit, the character has seconds to live. We'll cover that more in Chapter 9.

### Environmental
There are other, less spectacular, but still potentially exciting things that the environment can use to poke holes in your characters. Stationary objects such as the punji pit type mechanisms mentioned above, plants (either passively or

the more active varieties, for you science fiction and fantasy writers), insect stings and animal bites. In these situations, not only will the initial injury be a problem for your character, but as the story progresses you have the opportunity to introduce the effects of toxins and infection to twist plots and characters in whole new directions. Joy. A good many plant toxins have interesting, hallucinogenic, toxic, and deadly effects on people, but that's a subject for another time.

Being a science fiction reader myself, I've watched characters exposed to all manner of psychoactive and deadly plant products, both on the page and the screen, and I can assure you, the truth of the botanical world really is even stranger than fiction. In my own home state of Florida, for instance, there seems to be a never-ending supply of plants of various sizes (oleander bushes can grow to twenty feet tall) that come equipped with very formidable thorns, spikes, and needle-sharp leaves. Oleander thorns can be up to 2 inches long in full-grown plants. Many of these plants (still picking on oleander, here) are so poisonous that humans can't touch the sap or allow themselves to be exposed to the smoke from burning the cuttings. Not that I ever have, as Oleander is a protected species despite the fact it does a pretty good job of protecting itself.

Bites are a particular subgroup of puncture wounds, and if the bite is from a human, the site almost always becomes infected. That having been said, let's look at some examples.

Earth's surface and oceans are teeming with life, and in most cases that life comes equipped with a mouth. Inside that mouth we find—you guessed it—teeth. Grazing animals use teeth to crush and grind food and aren't likely to be interested in your character unless they've been abused, in which case they can deliver a formidable crush injury to your leading lady. Predators' teeth, however, are designed for puncturing, slashing and tearing flesh. Just sends a shiver of anticipation up your spine, doesn't it?

A colleague asked about including anaphylactic shock in this text, but I don't feel it's entirely apprpariate here unless your antagonist attacks your protagonist with bees or peanuts. Good luck with that.

# NINE

## BLOOD LOSS

*"When other little girls wanted to be ballet dancers, I wanted to be a vampire."*
—Angelina Jolie

**Blood Loss**

Blood loss is the process by which blood (hemoglobin, or the red stuff, and plasma, the straw-colored liquid part) leaves the heart and blood vessels and leaks into places it doesn't belong, like onto your character's garage floor. What we're talking about here is bleeding on a larger scale than your character cutting her finger with a kitchen knife while peeling a grape. A lot larger scale. There are lots of ways for characters to lose blood in the course of a fiction story. Some reasons come down to medical problems, like hemophilia, which we won't be talking about directly, or trauma, which we will, mostly because it's more fun.

What Kind of Traumatic Injuries Result in Bleeding?

Oh, let me count the ways. All of the injuries we've looked at earlier can cause bleeding, but let's recap. Your character can have an abrasion, or a scrape (think road rash) that may bleed but usually doesn't fully penetrate the skin. She may have an excoriation, which also is usually superficial and is more a scratch than a scrape. She may be cut, either a laceration or an incision, or she may have received a puncture wound or a ballistic trauma (gunshot or shrapnel wound). Any of these injuries can become major injuries if they penetrate the full thickness of the skin and cause a significant amount of bleeding. The two exceptions to this are ballistic trauma and blunt trauma from a nearby explosion. Almost any time a character is injured by a bullet or shrapnel, or an explosion, it will involve serious bleeding, and if the blunt trauma is significant (as it almost always is in an explosion), it almost certainly will produce bleeding, usually into body cavities like the chest or abdomen or into one or more extremities.

Blunt trauma causes injury via a shock wave effect that delivers energy over a large area. Wounds are often irregular and unbroken skin may hide a significant injury. Penetrating trauma follows the course of the causative device (knife, bullet, etc.). As the energy is applied in a more focused fashion, it requires less energy to cause significant injury. Any body organ, including bone and brain, can be injured and bleed. Bleeding may not be readily apparent as internal organs such as the liver, kidney, and spleen may bleed into the abdominal cavity and the lungs and major blood vessels coming from the heart can bleed into the chest. The only external signs of blood loss might be your character going into shock, especially if she's young. The cardiovascular system of young people tends to compensate well for moderate blood loss until they reach a tipping point. It's at that point that catastrophic collapse occurs.

Traumatic bleeding will usually result in fairly rapid blood loss. As we saw above, blood has two components; the red stuff and the liquid. Some of the symptoms of blood loss are attributable to each component.

## THE COMPONENTS OF BLOOD

### The red stuff
Among other things, the red component of blood contains hemoglobin that carries oxygen to all the cells in your character's body. If your character gets low on that, she will experience shortness of breath, rapid heart rate, fatigue, and possibly chest pain and muscle cramps.

### The liquid part of blood
The liquid part of blood is called plasma (no, this is not the same stuff as the purple glowing gas or your TV) is about 90% water and makes up

approximately 50% of your character's total blood volume (the red cells and white cells are the other half). Most people walking around are about 1-2% dehydrated and except for headaches and low-grade irritability, which they generally ignore, they don't even notice. Let's talk about that for a minute. Dehydration isn't exactly blood loss, but since water is the major component of blood, I think this is the most reasonable place to include it. Many of the symptoms of moderate dehydration are similar or identical to moderate blood loss, or hemorrhage, the difference is mostly how your character got to that point, which dictates what she will have to do about it (assuming that particular character is meant to survive).

If your character starts running low on volume (in the 5-6% loss range), she will begin to experience the symptoms of dehydration. These can include headache, dizziness, dry mouth and thirst, grogginess and sleepiness, weakness, nausea, and tingling in the extremities. Since humans have about 5 liters (1.3 gallons) of blood, these percentages represent quite small amounts of water. A loss of 5-6% equals approximately 250-300 mL.

At 10-15% loss, your character's muscles may start to spasm, her skin will start to wrinkle, her vision may dim, and if she can urinate, it may be painful. Losses greater than 15% could be fatal.

How your character got dehydrated will vary according to your story. She might be race walking across the Sahara or dogsledding to Pittsburg, or she might be stranded on a raft in the middle of the Atlantic after her boat sank, or even something as innocuous as spending a lot of time in a high-flying airplane (the air in aircraft at high altitude is in the neighborhood of 5%-12% relative humidity).

Doesn't matter.

That she's been without water for a day or two is what matters. People lose about two and a half liters of water a day just by being alive, sitting in a comfortable chair. That's more than a big soda bottle, only water. We lose water in vapor form during exhalation (approximately 350 mL), we lose water by urinating (oops, said it again—approximately 1000-1500 mL) and through defecation (150-200 mL), by diffusion through the skin (350 mL) and by sweating (another 100 mL). That loss is called insensible loss because we aren't even aware of most of the time, but it's still happening. In warm or humid weather, that water loss may increase tenfold. And your heroine needs that water replaced soon or she's going to be in trouble, which is right where we want her.

Let's do some quick math: if your character starts out with 5 liters of blood, that means she has about 2.5 liters of water as plasma in her veins. Okay, she will loose almost 2.5 liters of water a day just carrying out the business of life. That leaves her with... zero. Why, you might ask, does it take three-four days to get dehydrated enough to die? Because we have reserve water in our cells and between our cells, and the kidneys can become downright draconian about turning off the flow to the outside world in a pinch. But you're right, it's amazing that it takes as long as it does.

Mostly, though, for our purposes, the two component parts of blood can be thought of as one, 'cause that's how most of out characters are going to lose the stuff. And by the bucket-full.

A cut deep enough to involve the femoral arteries (located in the inner surfaces of the upper thighs) or the renal arteries (found at about the level of the bottom of the ribcage on the back and supply the kidneys with large amounts of blood) will cause your character to lose a fatal amount of blood in about 2–3 minutes.

### Shock

There are lot's of ways for a character to end up in shock, but for us, the most fun and relevant is *hypovolemic* shock from traumatic blood loss. Hypovolemia means "too little blood volume." It's different from dehydration, though, because, in blood loss, your character's body loses everything—hemoglobin, sodium, and potassium in addition to liquid volume.

**Stages of hypovolemic shock**

In the first stage of hypovolemic shock (up to about 750 mL), your character may look a little pale and experience some anxiety, but not much else. After about a liter of blood loss (about a quart in American), your character's heart rate will start to climb, typically above 100 beats per minute. Her blood pressure will stay normal, except the lower number, the diastolic pressure, will increase slightly because of blood vessel constriction to maintain pressure. She may sweat from the adrenaline released into her system to accomplish this.

For those of you who missed the amount or still just don't get the whole metric thing, let's put it in perspective—fill two empty 12 oz soda cans with tap water, go outside on a dry day, lie down on a large area like a driveway, and pour both cans onto your chest. Now look around at the size of the puddle. Feel how soaked your clothes are. Now imagine all that water is blood, and all that blood just flowed out of you and you can't stop it. You want to write scary stuff, write that feeling.

Stage II hypovolemic shock is 15-30% of blood volume loss (750-1500 mL). At this level, blood pressure is maintained but there is an increased diastolic (the lower number in blood pressure reading) pressure, her heart rate will increase slightly to around 100-120 beats per minute and her respiratory rate will increase slightly. Your character will also begin to perspire from sympathetic nervous system stimulation. Go back out onto that same dry driveway and pour a 1-liter bottle full of water onto your leg. Now, look at that puddle, pretend it's blood that just ran out of you. If you thought the exercise above was scary, this amount of blood loss is terrifying.

At stage III (1500-2000 mL), her blood pressure will continue to drop, her heart rate will climb to over 120 beats per minute, her anxiety will worsen and she will become confused and agitated. She will develop shortness of breath and fatigue, and her head will start to pound as well.

If your character continues to loose blood, at >2000 mL, her heart rate will soar to >140 beats/minute, her pressure will drop below the level required to maintain consciousness. Her headache and confusion will worsen, she will become lethargic (minimally responsive to all but painful stimuli), and her skin will become cool, clammy, and pale, and she will start to shiver uncontrollably. As things progress, she'll fall into a coma. Without treatment, she'll die.

Wow, that sounds like fun, doesn't it?

Another, slightly more gruesome method of separating your character from large quantities of blood is by detaching various body parts from him. Calm down, ladies, we're talking arms and legs here.

### Traumatic amputations fun facts
Outside of combat, traumatic amputations are relatively rare in humans (about 1 in 20,800 of population per year). Statistically, the most common causes, at least in civilized parts of the world, are from transportation crashes, industrial and agricultural accidents. Guns, explosives, fireworks, building doors, and car doors generally pick up the slack. So, when one of your characters threatens to jerk another character's arm out of its socket and beat him with it... nice sentiment, but not really feasible. Except for science fiction or fantasy, that is.

So, how much blood will your leading man (or any convenient victim) lose from parting with various extremities? Again, it depends. Arteries deliver blood under pressure, so blood loss can be incredibly rapid. In the good column, though, the arteries have evolved a mechanism that constricts them in the case of severe injury. If the artery is cut in a sharp manner, perpendicular to the wall, blood loss is slower than a crush injury or a ragged injury. In the case of a ragged amputation at the femoral artery (the big one in the upper leg), your character will probably lose consciousness in about half a minute, and without treatment, will most likely die in about 3-4 minutes. An arm would be a little longer, in the neighborhood of 45 seconds and 4-5 minutes, respectively. Veins are a low-pressure system but lack the constricting mechanism of the arteries. If the amputation/injury is further out in the extremities, your character will have a little more time, but he will be going into shock almost immediately.

Speaking of shock, an important point here is that emotional shock can cause an almost immediate loss of consciousness. The medical community refers to this form of shock as vasovagal syncope or plain ol' fainting. This form of shock is activated by some trigger, such as seeing one's blood running out onto the floor or significant amounts of acute pain, and is mediated by the brainstem, which tells the heart rate to slow, the heart's squeezing force, or contractility, to diminish, or the blood vessels in the body to dilate (expand) or, more likely, both. The result is a dramatic decrease in blood pressure that usually ends up with your character horizontal. Why your character's brainstem would do these things is beyond the scope of this text. The important part of this is that the result is the same—your character's blood pressure bottoms out and they end up on the floor. The difference is that your character will recover from vasovagal syncope fairly quickly (typically a few seconds) but not from passing out due to blood loss.

So, how long will it take your character to replace blood that is lost? As an example, let's use blood donation. Donating a pint of blood (450 mL) results in a depletion of about 10% of your characters total blood volume. Of that, approximately 160 mL are red blood cells. The remaining 290 mL of fluid is typically replaced within 12-24 hours. It takes the bone marrow approximately 3-4 weeks to replace the lost red blood cells, but the American Red Cross is very conservative in its donation guidelines (that's why people are not allowed to donate blood more often than every 6-8 weeks). If your character loses enough blood to go into the first stage of hypovolemic shock (up to 750 mL as noted above) it will take her 6 to 8 weeks to replace the lost red blood cells. Likewise, at about 1400 mL blood loss (stage II), your character is looking at a good 3 month's recovery time. Even at that level, though, with adequate fluid intake, she will be able to replace the lost volume in about 3-4 days.

# TEN

## STRAINS, SPRAINS & FRACTURES

*"I can't break anything because I don't have any bones."*
—The Scarecrow, *The Wizard of Oz*

**Sprain/Strain**
What Are Strains and Sprains?
Sprains and strains are injuries to soft tissues, either through injury or overuse.

What's the difference between a sprain and a strain?
A sprain will almost certainly hurt right away. After several hours, the injury will often swell and look bruised. It may be hard to walk or move the injured part. A strain, on the other hand, can start to hurt immediately (as in a pulled muscle), but more often, will take several hours to a day or two to hurt.

**Strains**
A strain is an injury to a muscle or tendon that attaches the muscle to a bone. Most skeletal muscles move the bones of the skeleton by contraction and relaxation. That's it. Contracting and relaxing. When a muscle contracts, it pulls on a tendon, which is in turn connected to your bone. Muscles are made to stretch, but if stretched too far, or if stretched while contracting, an injury called a strain my result. A strain can either be a stretching or tear of the muscle or tendon.

How does a strain happen?

As noted above, skeletal muscles contract and relax, and yet they move the body in an amazing array of directions. So, a strain is exactly what it sounds like—a muscle that's been stretched too far or too fast. It's common for people to strain the muscles in their backs, necks, or legs through overexertion. Strains often happen when a muscle is pushed too far, such as when lifting a heavy object. They're common for someone returning to a sport after the off-season. Muscles can also be strained by stretching them too fast. Inside every muscle are tiny stretch receptors whose job it is to monitor the change in muscle tension. If a particular muscle or group is being extended too rapidly, these receptors fire, causing the muscle to contract, slowing down the movement. It's a completely involuntary reflex, but if the force pulling the muscle exceeds the muscle's ability to counteract it, a strain can result. Finally, a strain can happen by pulling a muscle in one direction while it is contracting in the other (called an *eccentric contraction*).

Even though both can hurt a lot, strains are usually not as serious as sprains. Because a strain is pain in the muscle, it may start to hurt immediately or several hours later. The area will be tender and swollen and might even appear bruised. This is especially true if the muscle is damaged.

The exception to this rule is if the muscle or its tendon is completely torn loose (called a ruptured tendon or muscle rupture). Because all muscles come in matched opposing pairs (one to flex a joint, the other to extend it), all muscles are always in some small amount of tension or slightly contracted. This creates a balance until one rips free. This is a fairly obvious injury because the torn muscle will contract into a tight knot toward the end that's still attached, leaving a slight depression in the skin where it was.

This type of injury can happen to any muscle but it's a fairly common injury with some, like the long head of the *biceps brachii* muscle in the upper arm. That's the muscle that flexes the arm at the elbow. This tear causes a bulge in the muscle belly (the large, mid-portion of the muscle) sometimes called "Popeye Sign," but your character won't notice much weakness, as the slack is taken up by the other muscles around it. Your character will hear/feel a "pop" or tear, followed by significant pain. He probably won't be able to use that arm to lift anything for several days to a couple of weeks. Every time he moves the arm for the first few days, the pain will increase substantially.

Sometimes these tears are surgically repaired, but rehabilitation is long and involved, and the resulting repair is never quite as strong as before the injury, predisposing your character to a re-injury.

**Recovery**
Usually, strains don't result in long-term problems for characters unless they result in muscle tears. If the tear is incomplete (as in a few of the muscle fibers), they're painful (a deep, burning-type pain), and often result in swelling and bruising from blood leaking into the surrounding area. These bruises will typically take several weeks to resolve, just like all other bruises (see chapter 3). If the tear is complete, your character will sometimes require surgery to regain use of the muscle. Sometimes, as in the case of a biceps muscle, surgery is not required

**Sprains**
Bones meet at joints, such as elbows, knees, or shoulders. Strong, elastic bands of fibrous tissue called ligaments hold bones together at the joints. A sprain happens when those ligaments have been overstretched (mild sprain) or torn (severe sprain). Ankles, wrists, and knees are especially susceptible to sprains.

How does a sprain happen?
Ligaments can be injured by being stretched too far from their normal position. The purpose of having ligaments is to hold the skeleton together in a normal alignment—ligaments prevent abnormal movements. However, when too much force is applied to a ligament, such as in a fall, the ligaments can be stretched or torn. This type of injury is called a sprain.

What causes a sprain?
A sprain is caused by a ligament being stretched past its natural limit, known as being overextended. This can cause overstretching of the joints, or a tear or slipping of the ligament. Although any joint can experience a sprain, twisted ankles are probably the most common sprain. It has been said that serious

ankle sprains are more painful and take longer to heal than actually breaking the bones in that area. This injury often occurs in activities such as running, hiking, and sports that put twisting motions on the leg joints, like basketball or football. Your character may fall or step on an uneven surface and roll their ankle to the outside as the foot rolls to the inside. This stretches the ligaments on the outside of the ankle, called the *talofibular* and *calcaneofibular* ligaments.

Knee sprains run (pardon the pun) a close second to ankle sprains in frequency. Probably the most talked-about sprain is to the anterior cruciate ligament (ACL) of the knee. This can be a disabling sprain common to athletes.

### Classification of sprains
1. First-degree sprain - is a tear of only a few fibers of a ligament.
2. Second-degree sprain - is a tear of part but nor all of a ligament's fibers.
3. Third-degree sprain - is a complete tear of the ligament.

Sprains are commonly graded according to the extent of the injury. Grade I and Grade II ankle sprains can usually be treated conservatively with treatments such as rest, ice, and physical therapy. Grade III sprains can place individuals at higher risk for permanent joint instability, and an operation may be a necessary part of treatment.

This kind of injury can be immediately incapacitating for your character, with symptoms similar to a fracture, sometimes resulting in shock and loss of consciousness. Sprains are graded, as are most things in medicine. A Grade I sprain is where the tendon is simply stretched to the point of pain and irritation, sometimes with minor tearing. If these injuries occur to your character's ankle or knee, they will probably be unable to bear weight on that leg until the sprain heals.

### Dislocated Joints
Dislocated joints hurt just as much as broken bones and sprains. A dislocation is not necessarily synonymous with a sprain. A joint can be dislocated without

tearing the stabilizing ligaments. They can be forced back into place without medical facilities but it's not really recommended and will hurt a lot, probably enough to cause unconsciousness (vasovagal shock, Chapter 9). On-the-hoof treatment is the same as for broken bones—immobilize and support of the limb.

There are a few dislocations which can be life-threatening—the *sternoclavicular* joint (where the collarbone joins the breastbone) is one. It requires a lot of force to pop it (most people's collarbones will break before the joint goes), and the collarbone usually goes outwards, but if it displaces inwards, it can compress the airways. This joint can dislocate if your character gets slammed very hard into something like a wall and take the impact on the point of the shoulder.

**Symptoms**
Pain is the most common complaint. Sprains are often described as a sharp, stinging pain followed almost immediately by a deep burning sensation in the affected joint. The pain will typically increase immediately if the joint is moved or your character tries to put weight on it (in the case of a knee or ankle). She may become nauseous and vomit and may even pass out.

If your character's ligament is ruptured (either a Grade II or III), she may hear a popping sound at the time of the injury. This is a more serious injury and may be immediately incapacitating to your character. A few hours later, the injured joint will almost certainly develop considerable swelling and if there's damage to the ligament, a bruise will likely form in the area.

**Recovery**
Sprains can take quite a long time to recover from, depending on the severity (first, second, or third degree), the location (ankles and knees would obviously take longer to heal than, say, a wrist), and the treatment. Let's say, for example, your character sprains his ankle a week before the big game, and there are college scouts coming to watch. If his injury is relatively minor, he might get away with resting it and taping it for the game. He might then be able to play (in pain), but would probably extend the injury, putting his continued athletic

career in jeopardy. A complete rupture would generally finish him off and might require surgery to repair. The same is true of a knee injury. Making things worse is the extended recovery time for knee injuries because the knee cartilage has no direct blood supply, relying on nutrients in the joint fluid.

## Fractures

When a bone breaks it is called a fracture. Same thing. There's more than one way to break or fracture a bone. A break can be anything from a hairline fracture (a thin break in the bone) to the bone that's snapped in two pieces like a broken tree branch.

What Happens When a Bone Breaks

It hurts to break a bone, but it's different for everyone. The pain is often described as a deep ache or a burning sensation. Some people may experience sharper pain— especially with an open fracture. And if the fracture is small, a person may not feel much pain at all. Sometimes, people aren't even able to tell that they broke a bone.

Breaking a bone is usually a big shock to your character's whole body. It's normal for an injured person to receive strong messages from parts of your body that aren't anywhere close to the fracture. Your character may feel dizzy, spacey, or even chilly from the shock. Some people pass out until their bodies have time to adjust to all the signals they're getting and others don't feel any pain right away because of the shock of the injury. It all depends.

But even for those characters lucky enough to be in the middle of an adrenaline-soaked battle scene when they break their little toe and miss the initial pain, there will be a comeuppance later. Although bone tissue itself contains almost no pain receptors, a bone fracture is painful for several reasons:
- Breaking the continuity of the *periosteum* (a thin, plastic-wrap type fibrous fascial sheet covering bones, muscles, and muscle groups).
- Edema of nearby soft tissues caused by bleeding of torn blood vessels evokes pressure pain.
- Muscle spasm from trying to hold bone fragments in place.

# HURTING YOUR CHARACTERS

Bones are usually broken by blunt trauma (either a fall onto a hard surface or a sideways-directed blow by the proverbial blunt object). The initial sensations usually associated with this type of injury is a severe, sudden, sharp, piercing, knife-edged, penetrating pain at the site of the injury. This pain is due to the force of the injury on the superficial tissues (skin) and the initial tearing of the periosteum. As noted in Chapter 2, the nerve fibers in the periosteum, bone, and bone marrow are generally the A-delta, fast-conduction nerves (initial, sharp pain sensation), and slow conduction C fiber nerves (second, deep, burning pain).

Fracturing of bone and the surrounding injury to muscle and blood vessels will often cause local bleeding and swelling (physiologic splinting) in the area of the injury. The initial sharp pain is from the fast conduction nerves of skin, bone, and periosteum, the second, deep dull pain is because of the slower conduction nerves, and the third, throbbing, pressure sensation is because of swelling pressing against the arteries in the area, which also have sensory-conducting nerves. The fast conduction nerves tire easily, leading to the fading away of sharp pain, followed by the second dull pain (these nerves are less easily tired out). For more information, refer back to Chapter 2.

## Broken Bones

In general, they hurt. A lot. Any character with a broken bone (with the possible exception of the ribs which I'll come to in a minute) is going to know about it and not be very happy. Having said that, it is possible that a fracture might not hurt much at all if there's no displacement, and it may not be immediately obvious that the bone is actually broken.

The initial shock and pain are often enough to cause unconsciousness. Keeping the limb immobile will minimize the pain but any pressure or movement is going to be extremely unpleasant.

Severe breaks (compound fractures) can cause part of the bone to protrude through the skin, this will also cause blood loss, which can be severe enough to be dangerous. More on that below. Nerves and blood vessels can also be permanently damaged.

Smaller bones are obviously more likely to break than larger ones but I can assure you from personal experience that they hurt every bit as much and will usually stop whatever fun-and-games your character was involved in before they broke whatever, at least for your character.

Distinguishing between breaks/sprains is not always easy... Usually, lots of pain but some movement is a relatively good thing—it indicates 'just' a tear. Less pain but very limited movement is a worry because it can mean your character has snapped something and the joint can become unstable and will require surgery.

## Simple / Compound fractures
All fractures can be broadly described as:
- Closed (simple) fractures: are those in which the skin over the fracture is intact
- Open (compound) fractures, or those that involve wounds exposing the fracture to the environment outside the body, and may thus expose bone to contamination. Open injuries carry a high risk of infection.

## Simple fractures
A simple fracture in an extremity can cause your character anything from minimal pain to incapacitating pain and shock. It involves both A-delta fibers from the initial injury and C fibers from the periosteum (the connective tissue around the bone).
- Your character will probably feel any or all of these:
- Sharp, sudden, nauseating pain with a sickening "snap" or "crack" as the bone breaks
- Deep, aching or burning pain in the area of the injury
- Probably be unable to move the extremity
- Possibly numbness if nerves are involved
- Lightheaded or dizzy from shock (may pass out)

# HURTING YOUR CHARACTERS

## Compound fractures

A compound fracture involves a bone fragment poking through the skin (ick!).

**This is an immediately incapacitating injury, usually resulting in shock and loss of consciousness, and usually ending up with bone infections that are very painful and difficult to treat**

Also, breaking a bone in this manner almost ensures the character will be incapacitated and will probably require surgery, otherwise their injured leg won't heal properly. Historical fiction writers, this is why wounds, especially to the legs, routinely resulted in amputations prior to niceties like anesthesia and antibiotics. During the American Civil War, amputation was so common, there would typically be a pile of discarded legs and arms just outside the surgery tent. Amputation, including sawing through a bone or cauterizing a bleeding stump with an iron heated to 400-500 degrees, in an awake organism with a working nervous system is painful to a degree difficult to imagine by modern writers unless they've worked in livestock production, where dehorning and branding are routine.

Stuff you may not be aware of (fun fracture facts)
Any bone can be broken. Examples of fractures that can result in unexpected consequences for your character or the story are:

## The Skull

A skull fracture is a break in one or more of the eight bones that form the cranial portion of the skull, usually occurring as a result of blunt trauma. If the force of the impact is excessive, the bone may fracture at or near the site of the impact and cause damage to the underlying physical structures contained within the skull such as the membranes, blood vessels, and brain, even in the absence of a fracture.

While an uncomplicated skull fracture can occur without associated physical or neurological damage and is in itself usually not clinically significant, a fracture in healthy bone indicates that a substantial amount of force has been applied and increases the possibility of associated injury. Any significant blow to the head results in a concussion, with or without loss of consciousness (refer to Chapter 4).

## The Clavicle

The clavicle is the bone that connects the trunk of the body to the arm, and it's located directly above the first rib. There is a clavicle on each side of the front upper part of the chest. The clavicle connects at one end with the sternum (breastbone) and the other end connects at the *acromion* of the scapula (out there by the shoulder) which is referred to as the *acromioclavicular* joint. The clavicle forms a slight S-shaped curve from the sternal end, curving towards the rear on its way to the *acromion* of the scapula. Since you've probably just reached up and touched it, yeah, that bone.

Clavicle fractures occur 30-60 cases per 100,000 a year and are responsible for 2.6-5% of all fractures. These fractures occur twice as often in males than females. About half of all clavicle fractures occur in children under the age of 7 and it is the most common pediatric fracture.

As mentioned above, the clavicle protects the first rib and the nerve bundle and blood vessels under it. The clavicle would be the first bone to break from a blow directed down onto the upper chest/shoulder, followed by the first rib, underscoring the importance and vulnerability of the structures under them.

## Ribs

The first rib is rarely fractured because of its protected position behind the clavicle (collarbone). However, if it is broken, serious damage can occur to a large bundle of nerves and the blood vessels that run under it to the arm. Fractures of the first and second ribs may be more likely to be associated with head and facial injuries than other rib fractures. The middle, or 4th trough 10th ribs, are the ones most commonly fractured. Fractures usually occur from direct blows or from indirect crushing injuries and a fracture can occur anywhere along the bone.

## Broken/Bruised ribs

A rib fracture is a break or fracture in one or more of the bones that make up

the rib cage. Rib fractures are a special case, not only are they fractures, but they can become either compound by breaking the skin, or can puncture a lung causing it to collapse, resulting in mild to severe shortness of breath or lacerating the liver, causing hemorrhage resulting in shock. The bottom two ribs, called "floating ribs," because they don't come around and connect to the sternum can break, lacerating a kidney. Left unattended, either a lacerated liver or kidney will usually result in your character's death within a few hours. Your character will probably experience:
- Sudden, sharp pain
- Inability to take a deep breath due to pain
- Shortness of breath, possibly coughing up pink, frothy material due to punctured lung
- If a lung collapses, large amounts of air can replace the lung. Shortness of breath will become severe, followed by dizziness, tingling in the extremities, and unconsciousness.

The inability to take a breath is because the movement of the broken, sharp edges of the bone against the periosteum re-injures it, sending new fast-conduction sensations with each inhalation. Like most broken bones, a fractured rib can be expected to be incapacitatingly painful for up to an hour or so, depending on the individual, with immediate improvement (reduction of symptoms) over 24-48 hours, and gradual resolution of pain over the following 1-2 weeks with return to full, pain-free mobility in 3-6 weeks in most young, otherwise healthy people.

Potential complications of broken ribs
All sorts of nasty complications can arise from broken ribs. A lower rib fracture has the complication of potentially injuring the diaphragm, which could result in tearing of that muscle necessary for breathing. Rib fractures are usually quite painful because the ribs have to move to allow for breathing. Even a small crack can inflame a tendon and cripple an arm. When three or more consecutive ribs are broken in two or more places, the detached bone sections will move separately from the rest of the chest and a "flail chest" results.

For a start, a broken rib results in the same intense pain as any other fracture, though a character who has just broken a rib will also feel winded and uncomfortable. After a few hours, the pain may increase and breathing may become difficult. Problems can occur when the injured person is breathing only shallowly because of the pain and not expanding their lungs fully. A lung can collapse as a result, setting the character up for pneumonia. Broken ribs can also puncture a lung or even the heart with fatal results. At this point, there are two directions you can take your character's story—one is that the collapsed lung will eventually (a few days to a week or so) heal on its own and re-inflate to its normal capacity—problem solved for your character.

The other, more significant problem for your character would be that the collapsed lung will be so damaged that it cannot heal before enough air leaks into the character's chest cavity that the pressure starts to push the other organs (like the heart) off toward the opposite side. If the trapped air puts enough pressure on the heart, it will be unable to continue beating—not so good for your character. Two movies that come to mind that portray this sequence of events fairly well are; *Three Kings* (1999, screenplay by David O. Russell), and *Playing God* (1997 written by Mark Haskell Smith).

The breathing difficulties of a collapsed lung aren't what will get your character—that will typically pass in a few days if they're encouraged to move around and take deep breaths despite the pain—it's the potential for air pressure to build up in the chest, cutting off the blood flow to the heart. A severely punctured lung can result in death within 3-15 minutes if untreated.

**The Arm**
The bone of the upper arm (the humerus) has an anatomically weak spot where most fractures happen called the "surgical neck" of the humerus. A serious fracture here can lead to nerve damage in the arm resulting in numbness and/or paralysis, which may or may not resolve.

Forearm fractures account for 10-45% of fractures in children and almost half of all fractures in skateboarders. The two most common injury mechanisms include falling on an outstretched arm and defensive fractures, where the victim tries to fend off an attack using the forearm. Fractures of both bones of the forearm are a serious matter, potentially disfiguring or debilitating for your character, usually requiring surgery to repair.

## The Hand

There are approximately 29 bones in the hand and wrist together, 5 of which are called the metacarpals. The metacarpals lie in the region just behind the large knuckles (the far ends of these bones make up one-half of those knuckles). Boxer's fractures generally occur in the 4th and/or 5th metacarpal of the hand. More specifically, the fracture usually happens in the shaft of the metacarpal. It almost always involves one character punching someone/something. The mechanism is just what you'd expect from the name. In a properly executed punch, the force travels along the radius bone of the forearm through the second and third metacarpals to the point of contact. The problem arises when the wrist is angled so that the point of contact isn't the larger, stronger knuckles of the index or middle fingers, but the less developed ring and little finger metacarpals.

The symptoms are pain and tenderness in the specific location of the hand, which corresponds to the metacarpal bone around the knuckle. There may be a raised lump on the top of the hand where the bone has shifted at the break. When a fracture occurs, there may be a snapping or popping sensation. There will be swelling of the hand along with discoloration or bruising in the affected area. Cuts on the hand are also likely to occur. Movement of the bone may be limited due to the fracture and pain may be inflicted if movement occurs in the specified area. Lastly, there could be a misalignment of the finger.

## Femur

This is almost always an immediately debilitating injury. Also, because the bone marrow inside the bone produces blood, a fractured femur results in considerable blood loss as well as pain and the inability to bear weight.

## Tibia/fibula

These are the bones of the lower leg. Like the forearm, the lower leg consists of two bones. The larger bone is the tibia and it's the weight-bearing bone of the lower leg. At the distal (far) end, the two bones, along with the talus bone of the foot, make up the ankle. It's possible, indeed, it's more likely that your character will break his fibula before his tibia, but both bones can be broken at the same time if the injury's bad enough. A fairly common fracture is a small avulsion fracture of the fibula bone where the ankle ligament attaches. This usually results in a significant amount of pain and the inability for your character to walk without assistance. This injury normally resolves in 6-8 weeks, if your character stays off her leg (crutches).

## Foot

There are lots of little joints in the foot to dislocate, and lots of bones to break, All these injuries result in the same symptoms we discussed above, so there's no need to go over them again here.

There are certainly other, more insidious potential complications of fractures, but many of these would be about what you'd expect—vertebral fractures resulting in paralysis, etc. I did want to catch the more unusual properties of fractures and how they might affect your character and story in ways you might not have thought of.

Wow, that was a lot of breakage. As I said before, and it bears repeating—don't try to read the book through from cover to cover. This isn't that kind of book. It's a reference guide, and by necessity it's superficial, as hard as that may be to believe.

# ELEVEN

## BLUNT TRAUMA

The BLT of Fiction Writing

*"Ouch."*

—Wile E. Coyote, *Zoom at the Top* (1962)

**Fun Facts**

Blunt trauma is responsible for more than 100,000 deaths annually in the United States. According to the Centers for Disease Control and Prevention, approximately 118,000 accidental deaths occurred in the United States in 2005. It's also the most frequent form of injury in the real world, and the most frequent cause of death in males under forty (we can only assume it's not the number one cause of death in males over forty is because the herd is sufficiently thinned and not because we're that much smarter). Although, it seems to take most of us that long to discover the usual outcome of uttering the magic phrase "Hey! Watch this!"

Estimates of thoracic trauma frequency indicate that injuries occur in 12 persons per million every day. Overall, blunt thoracic trauma is responsible for 20-25% of all deaths, and a major contributor in another 50% of deaths. That means that at some point in one of your twelve books, some character is going to get hit on the chest, arm, or abdomen hard enough that we'll want to know about it. Reassuring, really, in a way.

**Blunt Trauma**

Getting hit...

Aside from the obvious risk of getting whacked upside the head (Chapter 4) or breaking bones (Chapter 9), there are assorted other injuries and complications which can arise in the course of pummeling your characters. One of the most fun (at least for us) is blunt trauma.

## What is Blunt Trauma?

Blunt trauma is routinely involved in cases classified as accidents and "misadventure", as well as in cases of suicide and homicide. Whereas other forms of traumatic death (e.g., gunshot wounds, sharp implement injuries) occur under a relatively limited number of circumstances, deaths resulting from blunt force trauma occur in a wide variety of scenarios. For instance, almost all transportation fatalities—including those involving motor vehicle collisions, pedestrians being struck by vehicles, airplane crashes, and boating incidents—result from blunt force trauma. Other deaths resulting from blunt force trauma involve jumping or falling from heights, blast injuries, and being struck by a firm object, such as a fist, crowbar, bat, or ball.

A quick word about the term "misadventure." This is where your character does something that seems really cool at the outset and fails to discover how crazy and dangerous it is until well after the point of no return. An example would be duct taping fireworks to a kitchen chair after reading about the Chinese emperor who tried to reach heaven in that manner, or tying three hundred helium balloons to a lawn chair and… well, you get the idea.

As you plan or write your story, blunt trauma is best thought of as the Rome of acute injuries. All roads lead to and away from it. Blunt trauma will almost invariably lead to some combination of the injuries listed elsewhere in this book. It's not at all uncommon, for instance, for blunt trauma to result in generalized bruising, under which may be found a fracture or two; a couple of lacerations, maybe an abrasion, and potentially damage to one or more of the internal organs, which may cause enough bleeding to result in shock. And if the damage is that severe, it's almost certain to have caused some level of head injury.

# HURTING YOUR CHARACTERS

Blunt trauma is a smorgasbord of injuries you can heap onto your character and almost as much fun as the dessert bar. You can, for instance, pick one from the explosion column, and take sides of fracture, concussion, and burns, and even top it off with a small piece of penetrating injury and a cup of blood loss, if you're still not full. Hmmm, must be getting close to dinner time.

In medical terminology, blunt trauma, blunt injury, non-penetrating trauma or blunt force trauma refers to a type of physical trauma caused to a body part, either by impact, injury or physical attack; physical attack is usually referred to as blunt force trauma, which is also a legal term, implying intent to do harm.

Blunt trauma injuries result from an impact with a dull, firm surface or object or, more rarely, the shock wave of an explosion. Individual injuries may be patterned (e.g., characteristics of the wound suggest a particular type of blunt object) or nonspecific. Although this chapter focuses mainly on external injuries, blunt force trauma may cause contusions and lacerations of the internal organs and soft tissues, as well as fractures and dislocations of bony structures (Chapter 9). The major types of cutaneous blunt force injuries are as follows:

**Abrasion:** A tangential scraping injury to the skin (epidermis or dermis and sub-dermis) that results from friction against a rough surface (an example of which is "road rash"—see Chapter 3 for more details).

**Contusion (bruise):** Hemorrhage into the dermis, subcutaneous tissues, deep soft tissues, and internal organs as a result of rupture of blood vessels following impact with a blunt object or surface (like getting socked in the eye—Chapter 3 for more details).

**Laceration:** A bursting or tearing of the skin or other tissues resulting from compression or stretching associated with impact by a blunt object or surface (Chapters 2 and 6 for more details).

**Fracture**: A break in the continuity of a bone  (see Chapter 9 for more details).
http://medical-dictionary.thefreedictionary.com/fracture

**Avulsion:** A more severe form of laceration in which the soft tissues, musculature, and/or bone are torn away from the normal points of attachment (Chapters 2 and 6 for more details).

These injuries are often seen in combination with one another. For example, scrapes are often found at the margins of lacerations. Scrapes, lacerations, and bruises are often noted adjacent to or overlying broken bones. You get the idea.

The degree to which your character will be injured by the effect of blunt trauma is roughly proportional to the amount of kinetic energy transferred to her body. The formula (yeah, darned physics again, sorry) about one-half the mass of the object multiplied by the velocity.

There are as many ways to assault and batter your characters as there are stories in the naked city (sorry, that's an obscure television reference, even for me), but I did almost skip the pun associated with battering our characters. The burn chapter is coming up and it's a great segue. Maybe I'll come back to it near the end. Okay, pressing on.

## On to the specifics
## Chest Trauma
Records describing chest trauma date back as far as ancient Egypt [circa 3000-1600 BC] and to the 5th century when Hippocrates wrote a series of trauma case reports, including thoracic injuries.

By far, the most important cause of significant chest trauma is the motor vehicle crash. They account for as many as 70-80% of thoracic injuries. Falls, pedestrians being struck by vehicles, acts of violence, and blast injuries also result in significant blunt thoracic trauma.

# HURTING YOUR CHARACTERS

Blunt chest trauma commonly results in rib fractures (refer to Chapter 9). You can also use direct lung injuries such as pulmonary contusions (bruised lungs) and cardiac contusions (bruised heart) to cause your character difficulty breathing. Your character can also puncture a lung (also covered in Chapter 9), or bleed into the chest cavity (Chapter 8). When these conditions get bad enough (as in the case of a tension pneumothorax), the heart and/or *vena cava* (that big vein that the blood uses to return to the heart) can be shoved to the side, causing closing off of the return blood flow to the heart, circulatory collapse, and potentially death for your character.

Sternal fractures are rarely of any consequence except for pain, just like any other broken bone, unless they result in cardiac injuries, and then they are.

Due to the elasticity of the rib cage, getting smacked in the chest can cause a person to fly backward some distance. Of course, this means they can bounce off of something else and hurt themselves that way, too. Pretty cool, when you think about it. At best, they're going to be winded and have difficulty breathing, which causes a certain amount of panic in most people. And it looks rather alarming unless you're an X-Man and some wanker bad guy throws you against the side of a building, then—hey, no problem.

Heavy blows to the back can damage the spine resulting in possible paralysis and death. Kidney injuries are also common when someone is hit in the small of the back. They can bleed and may shut down altogether. Kidney failure means the body can't clear certain waste products from its system, and if the waste products build up too far, coma and death can result.

### Abdominal trauma

Blunt abdominal trauma is a leading cause of illness and death among all age groups, the symptoms of which may not manifest for several hours after the injury. Abdominal trauma usually results from motor vehicle collisions (MVCs), assaults, falls, or recreational accidents. As in most things that end in physical trauma (usually because of impaired risk assessment), men are slightly more susceptible than women.

Internal organs such as the liver and spleen can also be damaged by blunt trauma and bleed as detailed above. Other organs which may be injured are the pancreas and the intestines. If the pancreas is damaged it may spill digestive enzymes which start to digest the person's own insides. Obviously, this is rather unpleasant and painful (a severe, burning, cramping pain). Damage to the intestines can result in blockages (causing dull pain, nausea, and vomiting), bleeding, and the release of bacteria into the bloodstream resulting in septic shock (high fever and delirium, followed by sudden drop in temperature and blood pressure—fatal if not treated) This can take 24 hours or more.

The usual mechanisms of injury can be broken down into three types: deceleration (where your character rapidly slows down, usually by hitting something solid, like jumping/falling from/being pushed off a building and doing a belly-flop onto the sidewalk), crush injuries (meaning something really heavy settling onto or some force squeezing your character at the mid-section—that whole King Kong/Fay Wray thing on the Empire State building comes to mind), and external compression, where something punches or runs into your character's abdomen—pretty self-explanatory (see Chapter 3 for the minor injury side of crush injuries).

So, what will your character feel in these instances? Anything along the spectrum from "not much" to knowing immediately he's in deep trouble. Classic deceleration trauma can result in tearing of any/all of the connective tissue holding your character's organs in place. I would guess an intense, dull ripping sensation would be pretty close. Maybe nausea with/without vomiting. Then, depending on what's torn loose, your character will probably bleed into their abdomen, resulting in all the symptoms associated with blood loss and shock we discussed in Chapter 8.

A crush injury would result in a building pressure localized to the abdomen, becoming gradually more intense, until some hollow organ lets go, causing sudden temporary relief, followed almost immediately by intense burning as digestive juices and bile get dumped into your character's abdomen. Hopefully, that didn't ruin your lunch.

The catchphrase for the third mechanism, external compression is "sudden and dramatic." So, for all you lucky boys and girls out there who have never had the pleasure of being punched in the stomach, this would be expected to be associated with severe cramping of the abdominal muscles (from the initial impact), shortness of breath from the sudden increase in abdominal pressure forcing air out of the lungs, possibly continued inability to catch one's breath because of muscle spasm of the diaphragm, and possibly some vomiting. See how much fun you missed?

Some first-hand knowledge on diaphragmatic spasm here—your character will lay on the floor helpless, listening to his own continuous, grunting exhalation until all, repeat all the air in his lungs has escaped. Then, he will lay there, paralyzed and unable to inhale for about three to four seconds (a very long 3-4 seconds, by the way), until the air rushes back in again and he curls up in a fetal position until the pain subsides. Did I mention that I taught martial arts? Interesting thing about it, as scary as it should have been, it produced a clarity of thought I have rarely been able to reproduce. I was sure I was going to die, and the process was completely beyond my control.

There's almost nothing your character can experience that will cause blunt trauma to the abdomen that won't hurt—a lot, typically. It will probably be moderate to possibly incapacitating pain, and will most likely leave him on the ground, cold and clammy, and out of breath while the bad guys are free to search his pockets or steal his new running shoes. If the trauma's mild, and due to a fall or a motor vehicle crash, he may recover enough to walk/crawl away, coughing and gagging, especially if his life depends on it, but he will be in a hurting place. This also describes what happens to a male who's been kicked/punched/kneed in the naughty bits.

A note to female characters: it's really hard to kick your assailant in the 'nads, because guys are all conditioned to see that one coming and flinch. Much easier to kick them in the side of the knee. And, as an added benefit, it only takes fifteen pounds of force to dislocate a knee from the side.

## Explosions

An explosion is a rapid increase in volume and release of energy in an extreme manner, associated with the generation of high temperatures and the release of gasses. High explosives result in a process called a detonation, the shock wave of which travels at supersonic speeds. Subsonic explosions, on the other hand, caused by low explosives, travel at speeds below that of sound and are created by a slower burning process, known as deflagration. The best way to compare the two conceptually is the analogy of a battery, which releases its energy more slowly than a capacitor, which releases its energy all at once.

Kaboom.

The most common artificial explosives are chemical, the most notable of which is gunpowder, invented by the Chinese and refined further in the form of nitrocellulose by Frederick Augustus Abel and dynamite by Alfred Nobel. While your characters are most likely to encounter chemical explosions, there are others, including electrical and magnetic, mechanical and vapor, and nuclear.

The speed of the reaction is what distinguishes an explosion from ordinary combustion. Unless the reaction proceeds more rapidly than the resultant gasses can be expended through the medium (air, water, etc.), no explosion will occur. In the case of chemicals, a reaction must be capable of being initiated by the application of shock, heat, or a catalyst and rapidly release light, heat, and gas. Given these guidelines, many substances not ordinarily classified as explosives can behave as such.

No matter the source of the explosion, though, the majority of the effect it will have on your character will likely come from the shock wave generated by the explosion itself and the heat from the burning from the rapid expansion of hot gasses. In addition to burns and the concussive force of the shock wave itself, if your character is exposed to a nuclear explosion, he will also absorb a good dose of radiation resulting in the expected burns and probably blindness.

Likewise, no matter the source of injury through blunt trauma, the typical recovery time would depend, to a large degree, on the underlying tissue damage.

The usual treatment for internal injuries is IV feeding, antibiotics, painkillers and sometimes surgery.
http://www.scribd.com/doc/106135828/Blunt-Trauma
http://en.wikipedia.org/wiki/Blunt_trauma

# TWELVE

## BURNS

*"I know what death smells like. Death smells like gasoline, singed hair, and fingernails. It smells like cooking meat. My meat."*

—Rasmenia Massoud, *Human Detritus*

If the previous chapter was about battering your character, this one is about frying. See, I knew I could work a bad pun in here somewhere.

A burn is damage to your character's body tissues caused by heat, chemicals, electricity, sunlight, radiation or friction. Scalds from hot liquids and steam, building fires and flammable liquids and gasses are the most common causes of burns. The minimum temperature required for producing a burn on human skin is an exposure of about 5 to 6 hours at 44°C (111°F) or about 65°C (149°F) for 2 seconds.

A burn due to a highly heated solid body or molten metal will produce skin reddening and a blister roughly corresponding in size and shape to the material used. What that means for your character, is that if she uses a hot iron to dissuade an attacker, she may well be able to identify that person later because they will have an iron-shaped mark somewhere on their skin.

Burns produced by direct flame may or may not produced blistering, but blackening of the skin and singeing of the hair are always present. Singed hair becomes curled, twisted, blackened, and breaks easily. Burns caused by kerosene, oil, or petroleum products are usually severe and produce blackened, sooty patches and have a characteristic odor. Burns caused by explosions of gunpowder are usually very extensive and produce blackening and tattooing of the skin due to unexploded powder particles having been driven into the skin.

Uncontrolled X-ray burns (i.e. from atomic/nuclear bomb blasts or antiquated radiography machines). Radiation burns vary from mild redness to moderate to severe irritation of the skin, shedding of hair and superficial skin and color changes of the surrounding skin. Severe exposure may produce burns with redness, blistering or irritation, or even ulcers with delayed healing and ill-formed scars.

Exposure to orrosive substances typically produce ulcerated patches that are free from blisters, the hair is typically not singed, and the affected skin typically shows distinct, uniform coloration. Strong acids tend to produce dark, leathery burns on the skin while strong alkalis cause the skin to slough and leave moist, slimy, grayish areas. Hydrofluoric acid and bromine cause death of the skin and underlying tissues. A good example of the effect of hydrofluoric acid on human tissue (as well as bathtubs, floors, and plumbing) is seen in *Breaking Bad*, season 1, episode 2 (Cat's in the Bag). If you do watch the episode, pay attention to the fact that Walter and Jesse are wearing gas masks during clean-up. This will give you an indication of the resulting odors.

"Flash burns" refer to thermal burns due to sudden, brief exposure to heat or flame. This type of exposure is common in explosions, ignition of fine particulate material (e.g., the dust inside grain elevators is extremely flammable) or upon ignition of highly inflammable liquids. In these cases, all the exposed surfaces are burned uniformly. Physics point: neither flammable nor inflammable (never have gotten the distinction between the two) liquids explode. Gasoline will extinguish a lit match. Gasoline VAPORS, however, will absolutely light up your life.

Burns from electrical exposure are due to resistance, primarily in the skin. Damage is mostly localized to the area of contact, but additional damage can be done to your character by electrical current traveling along the nerves and blood vessels, possibly burning them in areas not directly touching the electrical contact point. Physical marks can vary from none at all to severe tissue damage depending on the severity of the shock.

## TYPES OF BURNS

### Electrical shock

Hurts! At low currents, your character will experience a vibratory, tingling sensation that may be associated with rapid muscle contractions in the body part in contact with the source, known as in the medical community as fasciculations. These sensations will increase in severity in proportion to any increase in current, turning into an achy sensation and a steady, uncontrollable muscle contraction similar to a bad cramp (which, in effect, it is) that can be quite severe and leave your character achy and tired after the current is removed. As current increases, localized symptoms will progress to generalized, and become unbearable.

### Electrical injuries other than burns

Injuries caused by contact with electrical conductors depend upon: (1) the kind of current: alternating current (AKA house current) is 4 to 5 times as dangerous as an equal voltage of direct current from a battery (take that, Thomas Edison). (2) the amount of current: the amount of current that will flow through or over the body may be determined by the formula CV/R, where C is the current in volts and R is the resistance of the body in ohms. That means the flow of current through/over your character's body is inversely proportional to the resistance. Alternating currents of 10 mA (milliamps) cause pain and muscle contractions described above, over 60 mA (or 300-500 mA of DC current) are dangerous and can cause the heart to start beating erratically, a condition known as ventricular fibrillation, which can be deadly to your character. An alternating current of 200 or greater mA normally causes the heart muscle to stop completely and is usually fatal.

Ten milliamps is equivalent to 0.01 or one one-hundredth of an ampere and 100 mA is 0.1 ampere.

# HURTING YOUR CHARACTERS

There are several medical uses for electricity, including as a surgical tool for cutting and/or coagulation. An "electrosurgical unit" uses high currents (in the neighborhood of 10 amperes) at high frequency (500 KHz) with various amplitude modulation. A thin, flat, pointed blade is used for accuracy.

**Torture**

Electricity has been used as a torture device since the 1930s. Electrodes are either attached to your character's body at specific tender spots, or two electrodes in close proximity are touched to the skin. When high voltage and low current is used, your character can experience quite a bit of pain without any actual harm.

The various devices normally use a wand or rod that delivers a high voltage but low direct current (DC) electric shock to a torture victim. It typically has a bronze tip and an insulated handle and is connected by wire to a control box with a rheostat to raise or lower the voltage. Power is supplied by a car battery or by a transformer connected to a wall socket.

The victim is usually undressed and tied to a chair or table or hung upside down by the ankles. Often water is thrown over the victim to reduce the electrical resistance of the skin and to increase the effect of the shocks. The torturer applies its tip to sensitive places on the victim's naked body, such as the head, mouth, genitals, breasts and nipples.

The high voltage means the shocks are ample but the low current means they are less likely to kill the victim, enabling longer torture sessions and many more shocks to be given than with higher current torture devices. According to an academic expert on torture, Professor Darius Rejali of Reed College, early models used over 50 years ago delivered between 12,000 and 16,000 volts at a current of a thousandth of an amp. By comparison, the Taser and other modern electric stun devices used by police forces deliver many times that voltage. It's possible that more recent models use modern electronics for even higher voltage.

The use of these devices is illegal in most countries of the world. Your bad guy can decide to use this sort of device for several good reasons:

- It's portable and can be used without complex installation, for example in anonymous surroundings or in the victim's home.
- It's cheap.
- The low current means the torturers can make a single session of torture last longer, in the hope it will be more productive.
- It's easy to use—the control adjusts the severity of the shock and a rod enables the shock to be delivered precisely to the desired spot.

## Lightning

About lightning... From articles in Windpower Engineering and Development, lightning bolts carry between 5 kA and 200 kA with voltages that vary between 40 to 120 kV. So, without resorting to math, the average lightning bolt releases enough electricity in a few tenths of a second to power fifty average houses for an entire day. Yeah, that's impressive. It's also unpredictable (your usual wand-wielding wizard aside). So, if your character wanders out into the yard during a thunderstorm, holds a sword in the air, and shouts "By the Power of Greyskull..." he's probably not going to be happy.

Lightning is static electricity looking for a way to reach the ground. If your character happens to be in the path, almost anything can happen, from nothing, as in the electricity passes through him without effect, to burns anywhere on the body, to having part of an extremity (usually a foot) blown completely off, to stopping his heart, resulting in immediate death.

I once had a friend who claimed to have been hit by lightning no less than six times, with no harmful effects. Three of those were observed. In one instance, the bolt came in through a window, passed through her, and blew a land line telephone off a table. The phone and table were in the apartment of another mutual friend who was less than five feet away. Consider this an unusual circumstance, though, as most people end up more like the phone than my acquaintance. Just sayin'.

# HURTING YOUR CHARACTERS

**Burn Fun facts**

In the U. S., in the 1970s, about 9,000 people per year died from burn injuries. Those with burns over twenty percent of their body almost always died. Because of advancements in resuscitation, wound care, infection control, and nutritional support, that number has changed dramatically. Between 2000 and 2010, an average of 3,800 people in the U.S. died per year of burn injuries. Now, people with burns covering 90% of their body have a chance to live, albeit with considerable scarring and extensive physical therapy.

An estimated 500,000 burn injuries receive medical treatment yearly in the United States. According to the 2009 national burn repository, direct fire/flame is responsible for 43% of burns, followed by scalds (30%). Burns sustained in/around the home account for about 65% of all burn injuries with a mortality rate of 4%. Approximately 75% of deaths from burns and fires in the United States occur either at the scene or en route to the hospital. Amazingly, or not, 70% of people sustaining burns were male (no big surprise, since no woman has ever thought deep-frying a turkey was a good idea).

Pretty common, then. So, let's look at burns and your characters. There are three types of burns, graded according to their seriousness:
- First-degree
- Second-degree
- Third-degree
- Forth-degree (there's some disagreement regarding forth-degree burns)

First-degree burns are the most superficial of the burns. Your character's first-degree burn will cause damage only to the outer layer of skin (the epidermis). These burns tend to be dry, red and minimally to mildly painful, more of a discomfort or an annoyance. These burns are normally described in terms like "stinging," or "hot," and "throbbing." This injury is so common, that we would be hard pressed to find a person in a room of fifteen people who has never been in the sun long enough for their skin to get red and painful, or touched a warm pan or stove element in the kitchen. These are all examples of first-degree burns. First-degree burns typically take a week or less to fully heal.

They invariably heal with no scarring or residual problems.

Second-degree superficial, partial thickness burns damage the outer layer of the skin and the layer underneath (the epidermis and the dermis). The difference between first and second-degree burns is the depth. Clinically (that is, to the observer) the difference is that a second-degree burn blanches white with pressure and forms a fluid-filled blister. The symptoms associated with second-degree burns are almost identical to first-degree burns, except they tend to be a little more intense and longer-lasting, discomfort to a moderate degree, with the skin continuing to be sensitive to light touch for several days to a week. The blister usually breaks within a day or two of forming, exposing the very sensitive nerve-ending-filled dermal layer of the skin to whatever craziness you, as the author, can dream up. These burns tend to leak clear fluid and stay moist for several days after the blister breaks. There is also a small possibility your character will develop an infection because her skin's integrity is compromised. These burns usually take two to three weeks to heal and often result in pigment color changes that may take months or even years to resolve.

If your character's burn is slightly deeper (a second-degree deep partial thickness burn), there will be less blanching of the skin with pressure. The blister that forms will have pink fluid-like liquid inside instead of clear, straw-colored fluid. This is a more serious burn, often becoming infected, as the disruption of the skin to this degree can cause abnormal local immune responses. Scarring is also common and may cause your character problems moving an extremity if the scarring is over a joint. Hands are both the most vulnerable to injury and have more delicate skin on the dorsal surface (that's the side away from the palm). These burns may require skin grafting (yet another potential trauma for your characters).

Third-degree (or full-thickness) burns damage or destroy the deepest layer of skin, reaching down into the fat layer underneath. These burns appear stiff, dry, waxy, white, leathery, or brown. The burn itself is painless, although the skin around it will still have sensation and be excruciatingly painful. These are serious burns, requiring excision of the dead tissue, sometimes amputation of the damaged extremity, skin grafting, and usually rehabilitation therapy, both physical for the burn healing, and psychological counseling for the emotional trauma. These burns always scar and may take years to heal, if ever, because the involved skin never fully regains its former strength and resilience, even after repeated skin grafting. The movie Darkman comes to mind, except anyone burned that badly would be expected to have difficulty moving because of scarring, let alone fighting evil. Characters with this level of injury that survive will have altered personalities because of the emotion trauma.

The last and most dangerous and disfiguring burn is fourth-degree. There is some disagreement whether this level of injury represents a separate level. The National Institute of Health, for instance, includes destruction of muscle and bone, and amputation due to burn in third-degree, but the Mayo Clinic includes it as a separate level. This injury involves having a body part burned away or burned so badly that there is not enough viable tissue left for healing, and amputation is the only option. The area will look dry, blackened, or charred. This injury is painless except for the tissue at the edges of the burn, which, like the other serious burns above will be excruciatingly painful for your character. Your character will probably go into shock with this level of injury and may pass out or even wander aimlessly in a dazed state until they do pass out. Left untreated, this character will most likely die within a few days from infection. Even with treatment, the shock to this character's body and immune system will be so great that he may still die.

Burns can also be assessed in terms of total body surface area (TBSA), which is the percentage affected by partial or full thickness burns. First-degree (erythema only, no blisters) burns are not included in this estimate. Burns of 10% in children or 15% in adult (or greater) are potentially life threatening injuries (because of the risk of dehydration and the risk of hypovolemic shock, kidney failure, and infection) and should have treatment and monitoring in a burn unit.

The revised Baux score is based on data gathered from 39,888 burned patients using a logistic regression model (fancy mathematics). The Baux-R score generally used by medical professionals to determine when treatment is futile and comfort care only should be offered. This score is determined by adding the area of the burn (% total body surface area or TBSA) to the age of the patient. The presence of inhalation injury (yes or no) adds seventeen years to the score. A score of 140 or greater is considered non-survivable.

So, how will your character die from a burn injury?

As mentioned above, people usually die of dehydration, shock (either hypovolemic or neurogenic due to pain), kidney failure, or infection. Another important consideration, though, is smoke inhalation and damage to the airways. Theoretically at least, your character can experience minimal physical burns, only to develop significant shortness of breath and require hospitalization because of additional injuries.

# THIRTEEN

## HEAT & COLD

*"The heat made people crazy. They woke from their damp bedsheets and went in search of a glass of water, surprised to find that when their vision cleared, they were holding instead the gun they kept hidden in the bookcase."*
> —Kristin Hannah, *Summer Island*

*"The climate of Barrow is Arctic. Temperatures range from cold as shit to fucking freezing."*
> —Steve Niles, *30 Days of Night*

### HEAT INJURIES
#### Heat cramps
There are three heat-related conditions that your character may experience. The first, and least dangerous condition is called heat cramps. This is exactly what it sounds like. Heat cramps are muscle spasms that result from loss of large amounts of salt and water through exercise. This can be caused by inadequate consumption of fluids or electrolytes, (sodium or, more importantly, potassium). They often occur hours later, especially when relaxing. Heavy sweating causes heat cramps, especially when the missing water is replaced without also replacing electrolytes.

In hot weather, the body cools itself mainly by sweating, or by sticking one's head into the freezer. The evaporation of sweat regulates body temperature. However, with strenuous exercise or overexertion in hot, humid weather, the body is less able to cool itself efficiently. As a result, your character may develop heat cramps, the mildest form of heat-related illness.

Although heat cramps can be quite painful, they usually don't result in permanent damage. To prevent them, your character may drink electrolyte solutions such as sports drinks high in potassium during exercise or eat potassium-rich foods like green, leafy vegetables. FYI here, according to the World Health Organization, bananas don't even make the top one thousand sources of potassium. That was purely Chiquita marketing hype. Signs and symptoms of heat cramps usually include heavy sweating, fatigue, thirst and muscle cramps in the abdomen, arms, and calves. Prompt treatment usually prevents heat cramps from progressing to heat exhaustion.

Your character's best bet for treating her heat cramps is the same as preventing them; by drinking fluids containing electrolytes such as one of the sports drinks, getting into cooler temperatures, such as an air-conditioned or shaded place, and resting.

**Heat exhaustion**

Heat exhaustion is a condition the symptoms of which may include heavy sweating and a rapid pulse. It's the middle step of heat-related conditions your character may face—worse than heat cramps, but not as bad as heat stroke. Heat exhaustion is usually caused by exposure to high temperatures, particularly when combined with high humidity and strenuous physical activity, like walking across Key West on a sunny August afternoon. Without prompt treatment, heat exhaustion can lead to heatstroke, a life-threatening condition. Heat exhaustion is preventable, but not for our characters.

Besides hot weather and strenuous activity, other contributing causes of heat exhaustion include dehydration, which reduces your character's body's ability to regulate and maintain a normal temperature. Alcohol use can affect your character's body's ability to regulate his temperature. Also, overdressing, particularly in clothing that doesn't allow sweat to evaporate easily can have a significant effect. Symptoms of heat exhaustion may develop suddenly, or over an extended period of time, especially with prolonged periods of exercise. Did I mention Key West in August? Thought so.

So, what symptoms will your character experience if she develops heat exhaustion? Her skin may become cool and moist, and she may develop goosebumps, even when in the heat. She will probably notice severe thirst with a dry, scratchy mouth and throat, excessive sweating, dizziness, fatigue, faintness, confusion, giddiness and irritability, and a weak, rapid pulse and rapid breathing, dizziness upon standing, muscle cramps, clammy skin, nausea, and a headache.

These symptoms can be expected to gradually worsen as your character's situation deteriorates. As her symptoms of heat exhaustion worsen, she may stumble and fall, and even potentially become delirious or experience intermittent visual or auditory hallucinations.

**Heat stroke**

Heat stroke is the most serious heat-related illness. It is more severe and often follows untreated heat exhaustion. It's extremely dangerous and can be fatal. Heat stroke occurs when the body becomes unable to control its temperature. The body's temperature rises rapidly, the sweating mechanism fails, and the body is unable to cool down. Your character's body temperature may rise to 106°F or higher within 10 to 15 minutes. Heat stroke can cause death or permanent disability if emergency treatment is not provided.

How will your character know if she is experiencing a heat stroke? She may notice that her skin has become hot and dry because she has stopped sweating. She may have a rapid, strong pulse, a throbbing headache, dizziness, confusion, and nausea, possibly with vomiting. If she has the ability to take her temperature, or someone else does, her temperature may well be above 103°F. Untreated, this condition usually results in unconsciousness.

Additionally, symptoms of heat stroke include hot, dry, flushed skin with a lack of expected sweating, disorientation up to and including hallucinations, and abnormal blood pressure. Make no mistake about it, if your character starts experiencing these symptoms in the course of your story, she's in deep trouble.

*"And now for something completely different."*
— John Cleese, Almost every episode of Monty Python

**Cold Injuries**

Cold injuries are generally grouped under hypothermia. Your character need not be exposed to sub-zero temperatures in order to suffer hypothermia. Mild hypothermia is defined as a core body temperature between 95 and 90°F (35-32°C), and may involve shivering, mild difficulties with fine motor movement, such as manual dexterity due to the numbing effect on the hands as well as shivering. Your character may also experience mild mental impairment in the form of confusion or cognition difficulties, including the ability to count backward from 100 by sevens.

Moderate hypothermia occurs with core body temperatures between 82° and 90°F (28-32°C). At this point, your character's ability to re-warm herself will be limited because at core body temperatures below 86°F your character will begin to experience and altered level of consciousness, including slurred speech, staggering gait, decreased mental skills, or the reduction or lack of response to verbal or painful stimuli. Shivering generally stops and loss of consciousness is close at hand.

## Cold water
Your character's core body temperature will lower more rapidly if she is immersed or submerged in water.

## Chilblains
Also, extended immersion in cool water or air well above freezing can result in a cold injury referred to as chilblains. Symptoms are itching and swelling in the extremities exposed to cold. These symptoms can take weeks to resolve after a few day's exposure.

## Frostbite
Frostbite is the freezing of tissue and may only involve superficial tissues or may extend to the underlying tissues, up to and including bone. The onset and severity of frostbite may be affected by air temperature, wind speed, duration of exposure, and exposed area. Predisposing conditions, such as inadequate insulation from the cold or wind, immersion in water, high altitude, fatigue, poor nutrition, dehydration, alcohol or drug use, use of tobacco products, or underlying circulatory disease will make the situation worse. Frostbite can occur within minutes following exposure to extreme

temperatures, or even above freezing temperatures if there's a strong wind or if your character is wet or at high altitude. Frostbite usually affects the nose, ears, hands, feet, and cheeks first.

**Frostbite typically occurs in two ways**
Losing body heat. Frostbite can occur in conjunction with hypothermia—a condition in which your character's body loses heat faster than it produces heat, causing dangerously low body temperature. When core body temperature lowers, it decreases circulation and threatens vital organs. This triggers a "life over limb" response, meaning your body tries to protect vital organs with a mechanism much like the mammalian diving reflex we talked about earlier (Chapter 6), sometimes at the expense of extremities. When exposed to cold, your character's body will automatically constrict blood vessels at the surface of the skin, shunting blood away from the cold and toward the center of the body to keep your character warm—and alive. With decreased circulation to the skin, your character's core body temperature gradually lowers and eventually freezes—at about 28°F (-2°C).

The other way frostbite can occur is by direct contact with something very cold such as ice or metal, like your character putting his tongue on the flagpole on the coldest day of the year. Touching frozen metal or ice with any exposed skin and not just the tongue can lead to its sticking to the surface, though. Heat is rapidly conducted away from your character's body in these conditions by thermal conduction. Exposure to these substances will lower your character's skin temperature and freeze the tissue.

The mechanism of injury in frostbite is the crystallization of water within the tissues, typically between the cells, and by the resulting changes in electrolyte concentrations within the cells. Additional damage may be due to ice formation inside the cells, resulting in bursting and destruction of the cell membranes. Initial damage occurs during the freezing process, and further damage occurs during reperfusion and rewarming of frostbitten tissue.

**Stages of frostbite**
Like burns, frostbite is staged depending on severity. Also like burns, frostbite

is staged in three or four degrees. Because of the insidious nature of frostbite, your character may not be aware of the severity of the injury until it's too late. Typically, after the initial stages frostbite, your character is unlikely to feel any pain until the area is rewarmed. Body parts particularly susceptible to frostbite are ears, nose, fingers, and toes.

First-degree frostbite is also referred to as frostnip. Frostnip only affects the surface skin. Initially, your character will experience itching and a prickly pain in the affected skin which develops white, red, and yellow blotchy patches and becomes numb. Your character may also experience clumsiness due to joint and muscle stiffness. Frostnip rarely results in permanently damaged skin, as only the top layers are affected. Occasionally, long-term insensitivity to both heat and cold can happen after suffering from frostnip.

If freezing continues, your character's skin may freeze and begin to harden. The skin may feel firm but not hard as the tissue under the skin has not frozen. In second-degree frostbite, your character's skin will initially turn red and as frostbite proceeds, will become numb. At this stage, the deeper tissues are still not affected and remain viable. The injured areas usually form blisters 1-2 days after being frozen. The blisters that form may become hard and blackened, but usually appear worse than they are. At this level of exposure, most injuries heal in approximately 4 to 6 weeks, but the area may become permanently insensitive to both heat and cold.

In third-degree cold injury, deep frostbite occurs. The muscles, tendons, blood vessels, and nerves all freeze. The skin turns increasingly pale eventually turning white or faint blue, becomes hard, and will not rebound when pressed. It will feel waxy to the touch, and sensation in the area is lost. In severe cases, your character may lose some of the use of the extremity permanently. Deep frostbite usually results in areas of purplish blisters which contain blood and turn black in a short time. This indicates that the frostbite has partially or totally thawed. Nerve damage in the area can result in permanent loss of feeling. Usual treatment for this level of injury is amputation of the affected part.

# HURTING YOUR CHARACTERS

Fourth-degree frostbite involves an extremity going though all the preceding stages. Eventually, the extremity turns black, stiffens, and freezes solid. Fourth-degree frostbite invariably involves loss of tissue through auto-amputation (the affected part(s) fall off).

# FOURTEEN

## DECOMPRESSION, DIVING ACCIDENTS & EXPOSURE TO VACUUM

Diving disorders are medical conditions specifically arising from exposure to increased pressures, as in underwater diving. Symptoms of these illnesses may present either during a dive, upon surfacing from a dive, or up to several hours after a dive. Because the ambient pressure underwater increases by one standard atmosphere for every 10 m (33 feet) of depth, your characters have to breathe oxygen/nitrogen mixtures at much higher pressures than at the surface.

In order to mitigate the effects of breathing gas at high pressures for extended periods, various mixtures of oxygen and other gasses are available. Nitrox, for example, is a mixture of a higher percentage of oxygen and less nitrogen to reduce the risk of decompression sickness at recreational dive depths of up to about 40 m (130 feet). In addition, helium may be added to reduce the amount of oxygen and nitrogen, allowing safer dives to deeper depths. Dives beyond 150 m (500 feet) become complicated because helium-oxygen mixtures (heliox) can cause high-pressure nervous syndrome.

So, let's see what trouble our characters can get into.

### Decompression sickness

When your character breathes an oxygen/nitrogen mixture (a.k.a. air) under pressure, the oxygen is used in metabolism, but the nitrogen isn't. It's retained in body tissues in a dissolved state, but at higher than usual concentrations. When the pressure is reduced, as in returning to the surface, the dissolved nitrogen is released from the tissues back into the bloodstream to be transported to the lungs where it can be exhaled. When a diver returns to the surface too quickly, the trapped nitrogen is released into the bloodstream more quickly than it can be removed from the bloodstream, forming bubbles. The resultant symptoms range from joint pain where the bubbles form, to blockage of an artery leading to the brain, causing stroke-like damage to the nervous system including paralysis, to the lung, resulting in damage there (Pulmonary barotrauma) leading to shortness of breath or death, or to the heart, resulting in a heart attack.

While bubbles can form anywhere in the body's bloodstream, musculoskeletal symptoms occur approximately 90% of the time, according to the U.S. Navy, while neurological symptoms occur in approximately 10 to 15% of cases.

Musculoskeletal symptoms of decompression sickness most often occur in the shoulders, elbows, knees, and ankles and include localized deep pain ranging from mild to excruciating, sometimes as a dull ache and rarely as a sharp pain. This pain is aggravated by any movement of the joint and may be reduced by bending the joint to find a comfortable position (hence the name, "the bends"). Onset of symptoms can begin up to hours after the character returns to the surface.

Symptoms of decompression sickness your character may experience in the skin include itching, especially around the ears, face, neck, arms and upper torso. Your character may experience altered sensation, including numbness or tingling, or increased sensitivity. Her symptoms may also include a sensation of insects crawling on the skin (formication—spelled with an "m"), swelling, and subcutaneous crepitus (a crackling sound) when the skin is pressed. This is due to numerous bubbles forming under the skin.

Neurologic symptoms, including headache, confusion or memory loss, visual abnormalities, unexplained mood or behavior changes, seizures or unconsciousness could be a problem for your character during decompression sickness. Your character could also experience weakness or paralysis in the legs, which moves from the extremities toward the body; abdominal or chest pain; and urinary or fecal incontinence if nitrogen bubbles form in the canal and put pressure on the spinal cord.

If your character's inner ear is affected, she could experience dizziness, vertigo, nausea, vomiting, or hearing loss. Pulmonary symptoms include dry persistent cough, burning chest pain aggravated by breathing, and shortness of breath. Pulmonary barotrauma is the second most common cause of death while diving.

These symptoms could resolve within a few hours if very minimal, but usually not. More commonly, symptoms will persist for days to weeks because the bubbles have become trapped, or may be permanent because of any resulting damage. The only two treatments for decompression sickness are to put your character in a pressure chamber where the nitrogen may return to a dissolved state, and slowly decrease pressure over days, or crawl into bed, cross her fingers, and hope for the best.

What else can happen?

### Nitrogen narcosis
Nitrogen narcosis is a decrease in the diver's cognitive ability poor motor skills due to the pressure of dissolved nitrogen within the brain itself. If your character experiences nitrogen narcosis, she may not recognize the symptoms in herself because of the condition's perception-altering ability. The effects vary widely from day to day in the same individual and from individual to individual. As depth increases, mental impairment may become hazardous. Divers can learn to cope with some of the effects of narcosis, but it's impossible to develop a tolerance.

Nitrogen narcosis, also known as inert gas narcosis, raptures of the deep, or the Martini effect, is a reversible alteration in consciousness that occurs while diving at depth. It is caused by the anesthetic effect of certain gasses at high pressure. The Greek word narcosis is derived from narke, "temporary decline or loss of senses and movement, numbness" and originally used by Homer and Hippocrates. Narcosis produces a state similar to drunkenness (alcohol intoxication), or nitrous oxide inhalation. It can occur during shallow dives, but doesn't usually become noticeable at depths less than 30 meters (100 ft).

Narcosis may be completely reversed in a few minutes by ascending to a shallower depth, with no long-term effects. Thus narcosis while diving in open water rarely develops into a serious problem as long as the divers are aware of its symptoms and are able to ascend to manage it. Diving much beyond 40 m (130 ft) is generally considered outside the scope of recreational diving.

**High-pressure nervous system syndrome**
Of all the available gasses, helium causes the least side effects at high pressures. However, at depths of approximately 500 feet, symptoms such as tremors and difficulty with fine motor movements, especially manual dexterity, are reported.

**Oxygen toxicity**
Oxygen toxicity results in convulsions, resembling epileptic seizures. These seizures are often preceded by a telltale sensation described as "a strange light, zigzag lines, vibrating visual field, darks spots, modification of voices, an unpleasant smell or confusing thought," known as an aura similar to the aura associated with some migraines. At concentrations greater than normal, oxygen overwhelms the bodies normal antioxidants, becoming toxic. The lungs and brain are particularly vulnerable to oxygen toxicity encountered during diving. Normally, oxygen makes up 20% of the 16 pounds per square inch (PSI) we breathe at sea level or about 3.2 PSI total. Partial pressures of oxygen around 7.3 psi can be tolerated by people indefinitely, and up to 20 PSI for many hours.

**Human exposure to a vacuum**
There are essentially two ways your character can find herself in this predicament: having a spaceship or spacesuit spring a leak, or being flushed out of an airlock. This is referred to as "spacing" in the *Babylon 5* series and

"airlocking" in *Battlestar Galactica*. What really happens to a character exposed to a vacuum? Some really bad things, including:

**Oxygen deprivation**

Oxygen deprivation is first and foremost. Apart from the obvious—lack of oxygen is bad for your character (6-8 minutes for permanent brain damage)—the reason for the lack can have side effects of its own. For example smoke, chemical or water inhalation can do physical damage to the lungs making breathing difficult even when the person is removed to a safe place.

Exposure to the decreased pressure of a vacuum

Less than 50% atmospheric pressure can have people suffering from hypoxia (oxygen deprivation). At less than 15%, your character may as well be in vacuum—meaning that holding her breath would be a Big Mistake, but not one she'd live to regret for very long. Assuming your character survived the initial decompression, she'd have about 10 seconds of consciousness to do something about it and about a minute and a half to live. Parts of the body exposed would suffer from swelling and interrupted circulation.

Possibly, the most well-known scene about exposure to a vacuum is that one from *2001: A Space Odyssey* where astronaut Dave Bowman jumps from the pod to the *Discovery* without a helmet. The most frequently asked questions are: How realistic is that scene? How long could a human survive if exposed to vacuum? Would my character explode? Would he survive? How long would he remain conscious?

The quick answers to these questions are: Pretty close, about ninety seconds, he wouldn't explode, no, and he would remain conscious for about ten seconds. And now for the long answers:

How realistic is that scene?

Probably the most realistic part of that scene was the absence of sound. Sound needs a medium in which to travel, air works fine, water works better, and a vacuum works not at all. In a vacuum, there are no molecules to carry the sound wave. Another part of that scene that was particularly authentic, was that what little air did accompany Dave was almost immediately dissipated in all directions after taking him through the hatchway. The one disappointment of that scene, though, was that Dave didn't sustain quite enough injury from even the brief exposure to vacuum. Even in the reduced atmosphere of the spaceship and pod, the exposure to vacuum would have caused some burst blood vessels in the whites of his eyes and probably would have resulted in his coughing up a small amount of blood from mild barotrauma to the lungs.

How long could a human being survive if exposed to a vacuum?

According to the chapter on the effects of Barometric pressure in Bioastronautics Data Book, Second edition, NASA SP-3006, some degree of consciousness will probably be retained for 9 to 11 seconds. Your character would actually have between 5 and 10 seconds to help himself. In rapid sequence thereafter, paralysis will be followed by generalized convulsions and paralysis. During this time, water vapor will form rapidly in the soft tissues and somewhat less rapidly in the venous blood. This evolution of water vapor will cause marked swelling of the body to perhaps twice its normal volume unless it is restrained by a pressure suit, while venous pressure rises due to distention of the venous system by gas and vapor. Venous pressure will meet or exceed arterial pressure within one minute. Then, there will be virtually no effective circulation of blood. Once heart action ceases, death is inevitable despite any attempts at resuscitation. Your character would die within a minute to a minute and a half after exposure to a total vacuum. After an initial rush of gas from the lungs during decompression, gas and water vapor will continue to flow outward through the airways. This continual evaporation of water will cool the mouth and nose to near-freezing temperatures, much the way releasing the pressure on a can of compressed air causes condensation and frost to form around the opening. The remainder of the body will also cool, but more slowly.

Would my character explode?

No, unfortunately for Hollywood your character will not explode if exposed to near total or total vacuum. It seems that skin is much more pliable and tougher stuff than we often give it credit for. Your character's skin will not split open, and they will not explode, throwing goo all over the inside of the spaceship or cluttering up the universe. What will most likely happen is unless restrained by a space suit, your character will expand to about twice their normal volume, and superficial blood vessels will burst. This will most likely be quite painful for your character.

In 1960, during a high-altitude balloon parachute jump, a partial-body vacuum exposure incident occurred when Joe Kittinger, Jr. lost pressurization in his right glove during an ascent to 103,000 ft (19.5 miles) in an unpressurized balloon gondola, Despite the depressurization, he continued the mission even though the hand had become painful and useless. After he returned to the ground his hand returned to normal. Kittinger wrote in *National Geographic* (November 1960):

"At 43,000 feet I find out [what can go wrong]. My right hand does not feel normal. I examine the pressure glove; its air bladder is not inflating. The prospect of exposing the hand to the near-vacuum of peak altitude causes me some concern. From my previous experiences, I know that the hand will swell, lose most of its circulation, and cause extreme pain.... I decide to continue the ascent, without notifying ground control of my difficulty."

At 103,000 feet, he writes: "Circulation has almost stopped in my unpressurized right hand, which feels stiff and painful."

But at the landing: "Dick looks at the swollen hand with concern. Three hours later the swelling will have disappeared with no ill effect." The decompression incident on Kittinger's balloon jump is discussed further in *Shayler's Disasters and Accidents in Manned Spaceflight*:

[When Kittinger reached his peak altitude] "his right hand was twice the normal size... He tried to release some of his equipment prior to landing, but was not able to as his right hand was still in great pain. He hit the ground 13 min. 45 sec. after leaving Excelsior. Three hours after landing his swollen hand and his circulation were back to normal."

See also from Leonard Gordon, *Aviation Week*, February 13, 1996.

Could my character survive?

If your character can restore air pressure (to higher than about 3.5-4 PSI) within 30 to 60 seconds, they will begin to breathe again and although experiencing some minor injuries, would most likely recover rapidly and survive. There are several cases of humans surviving exposure to vacuum worth noting. In 1966 a technician at NASA Houston was decompressed to vacuum in a space-suit test accident. This case is discussed by Roth in the reference above. He lost consciousness in 12-15 seconds. When pressure was restored after about 30 seconds of exposure, he regained consciousness, with no apparent sustained injury.

Please note that in every instance we've covered, I've specified exhaling immediately upon exposure. Sudden decompression can have disastrous effects if the person involved makes the mistake of trying to hold his or her breath. This will inevitably result in severe rupture of the lungs, with almost certainly fatal results. It's called "explosive" decompression for a reason.

Will my character's blood boil?

No.

Her blood is at a higher pressure than the outside environment. A typical blood pressure for your character might be 120/76. The "76" part of this means that between heartbeats (see chapter 8), the blood is at a pressure of 76 Torr (approximately 1/10th atmospheric pressure) above the external pressure. If the external pressure drops to zero, at a blood pressure of 76 Torr, the boiling point of water is 46 degrees Celsius (115 F). This is well above body temperature of 37 C (98.6 F). Her blood won't boil because the elastic pressure of her blood vessels keeps it at a pressure high enough that the body temperature is below the boiling point—at least until her heart stops beating, at which point she'll have other things to worry about.

Would your character freeze?

No. Sorry.

A few recent Hollywood films and many older novels depicted people instantly freezing solid when exposed to a vacuum. Often, one of the egg-headier scientist characters would mention that the "outside" temperature was "minus 273"— that is, absolute zero, or state that the temperature is "zero degrees kelvin" (the kelvin is not referred to or typeset as a degree, it's an absolute number).

But in a practical sense, space doesn't really have a temperature—you can't measure a temperature in a vacuum because there's nothing there to measure. The residual molecules that do exist aren't close enough to have much of any effect. Space is neither "cold" nor "hot." It isn't anything.

What space is, though, is a very good insulator (a vacuum is the secret behind thermos bottles). What we see too often is misinformed sci-fi wannabe writers blathering on about "the cold depths of space" or "the freezing void," which may be poetic and picturesque, but is repeated so often that if not used in a story, it could be met with disbelief by the reader.

If your character were exposed to space without a spacesuit, her skin would most likely feel slightly cool, due to water evaporating off her skin, leading to a small amount of evaporative cooling. But she wouldn't freeze solid. Again, there's other stuff for her to worry about.

**Explosive Decompression**
The discussion here has focussed only on exposure to vacuum. However, in general, the action of being exposed to vacuum will also involve a rapid

decompression. This event is generally known as *explosive decompression*, and apart from the simple effect of vacuum on the body, the explosive decompression event itself will be hazardous. As noted, explosive decompression will be particularly bad if the decompression subject attempts to hold his or her breath during said decompression.

**A note here on throwing characters out an airlock:**
As much fun as it might be, simply throwing someone out of a spaceship or a space station's airlock without a suit, or as it's known in some novels and movies, "spacing," or simply "airlocking," as a method of killing someone in sci-fi works involving space travel is usually reserved as a last-ditch effort to get rid of a character or body. Certain captains (especially space pirates) have been known to use this as a method of execution. A somewhat crueler version involves giving the executed a spacesuit with enough air to let them last a while so they can fully appreciate their upcoming death.

An odd bit of Hollywood science regarding getting thrown out of an airlock is that it always causes the victim to be violently sucked out into space. In real life, a pressure difference of a single atmosphere would not cause very much suction and would happen almost instantly rather than cause the prolonged gale-force winds that seems to always happen in the movies. Granted, there would be a rather fast stream when the hatch starts to open, but by the time it opens enough for someone to exit, the wind will have slowed down considerably. As airlocks are, in the vast majority of cases, intended for scenarios other than tossing someone out of, they will likely be designed to minimize air loss. This includes having air lock chambers as small as possible and some foolproof measures to ensure that both doors will not open at once. Which means there's simply not enough air to be dramatic. Also, there's no reason to give any airlock a powerful instantly-opening door if it's not an evacuation exit or torpedo tube—it's more likely to have the air slowly pumped out (or, more likely, pumped back into the ship) before opening, especially since in a spaceship traveling through a vacuum, air becomes a very precious commodity, unlikely to be wasted using it to flush characters into the Kuiper belt.

# MICHAEL J. CARLSON

In Ben Bova's *Venus*, Captain Fuchs places rebelling crew members onboard a faulty escape pod and ejects it, leading to an extremely painful and messy explosive decompression.

Robert A. Heinlein uses this technique in *The Moon Is A Harsh Mistress*, except, in this case, the airlock is the city's, and not a spaceship. Also, one of the heroes of *Rocket Ship Galileo* threatens to do this to a Nazi prisoner to get him to talk.

In *Chasm City* by Alastair Reynolds, two incompetent medics accused of causing the death of their captain are executed this way, with the air being slowly vented from the airlock to increase their suffering.

Larry Niven's work tends to subvert this concept fairly often, making the vacuum of space relatively easy to deal with, usually by not having the pressure drop from "normal" to hard vacuum in a fraction of a second unless the hole is pretty big.

# FIFTEEN

## UNREALISTIC RECOVERY TIME

*Imagination is more important than knowledge. "*

—Albert Einstein

Between them, "Hollywood Healing" and "Made of Iron" cover the two main varieties of action hero—the hero who seems to be able to walk unscathed through a bomb-blast, and the one who gets hurt badly but somehow always manages to come back and triumph in the end.

Although movies are the worst offenders, the world of literature is attempting to catch up with a phenomenon known as Hollywood Healing. While it predominantly affects the action-adventure saga, Hollywood Healing has a tendency to bleed over into other genres as well (pun intended). It works like this: no matter how badly he's injured, whether from a gunshot, blade, or explosion, and action-adventure hero never ends up with a scar anyplace visible (Although he may have one or 2 hidden under his shirt which he can take off to reveal just how manly he really is). Additionally, no matter how serious an injury is, the main character can be counted on to exhibit full recovery, usually within a few scenes (these scenes usually show the character in physical therapy, rapidly improving).

**Examples in film**
The Stephen Seagal movie *Hard to Kill*, is a particularly egregious offender. The main character, Los Angeles Police Detective Mason Storm not only

survives a seven-year long coma but is able to realize that he is still in danger and drags himself to an elevator to escape with the assistance of nurse hottie Kelly LeBrock. Over the next few days, Storm uses his knowledge of meditation techniques, acupuncture, moxibustion, and martial arts to fully recover his strength, all while still grieving the death of his wife, which he only became aware of upon awakening from his coma and completely ignoring nurse hottie.

Except for the 1963 film, From *Russia With Love*, which portrayed the usually unstoppable James Bond with something close to realistic injuries after getting his backside handed to him. Throughout the 80s and 90s, however, it seemed that no matter how desperate the altercation, the James Bond character never developed a black eye, a broken nose, or a visible bruise until *Casino Royale* (2006), which treated viewers to a return to a grittier Bond with facial abrasions and excoriations. Wonder how he got that scalp laceration he sustained battling a machete-wielding adversary down a stairwell to heal before he returned to the high-stakes poker game? Hmmm.

In the movie *Eraser*, Arnold Schwarzenegger uses a refrigerator door as a shield to protect against a grenade that fires straight spikes of metal, one of which impales his right hand between the knuckles of the index and middle finger to the door. After he pulls his hand free of the spike, his injury fails to affect the dexterity of that hand for the rest of the film.

In the original *Shaft*, the title character is shot in the shoulder at close range by a machine gun. He hits the floor, apparently unconscious, and after minimal medical attention gets right back into action.

The *Darkman* movies have a particularly blatant example of Hollywood Healing. The evil character Durant is killed on a helicopter when it explodes during the first movie. In the second movie, he returns with a limp, but alive with no scarring or disfigurement. Durant's survival may have been a retrofit of past events to serve a current plot need (similar to the dreaded deus ex machina), but it's still very jarring when you consider that the main character's disfiguring scars also came about because of an explosion, caused by Durant.

# HURTING YOUR CHARACTERS

During a joust in the movie, *A Knights Tale*, William, the main character, as is stabbed in the shoulder with a lance. The tip breaks off inside, causing sufficient injury that he can no longer grip his own lance unaided. As soon as he wins the competition though, he is able to dismount without difficulty and fiercely hug his love interest, the fair Jocelyn. No further mention of the wound is made, proving once and for all that injuries were not debilitating and infection was not a really problem seven-hundred years before surgical care or antibiotics.

A phenomenon closely related to Hollywood Healing is Made of Iron. Simply put, damage is done to characters that really should hurt them but is of no significance to the character. Nobody ever breaks a rib or other bones unless that specific injury becomes an important plot point later on. Note, this isn't the same condition as where the character actually is supernaturally protected from harm. This is the ability to shrug off blows that would normally incapacitate or kill a human being.

By extension, blunt damage, concussions, and other side effects of "non-lethal" fights never have unintended consequences—serious injury or death can only happen with intentionally, e.g. by lethal weapons like swords or guns. And even with normally lethal weapons, the hero may at any time inflict nonlethal flesh wounds instead of shooting to kill.

One especially tenacious example is the lack of loss of long-term cognitive skills despite repeated head injuries. Nancy Drew and Jimmy Olsen were knocked unconscious several times in of any of hundreds of adventures with no long-term brain damage to show for it (okay, Jimmy was kind of goofy toward the end). Indeed, unrealistic lack of lasting damage from serious head injuries is widely prevalent in movies and literature.

The term "Punch-drunk" is historically applied to boxers as the classic real-life example of what happens to someone who experiences repeated head trauma in many fights year after year. The American National Football League provides a better example of the repercussions of a very physical life. More than a few seasons of pro football guarantee a player a life expectancy about ten years shorter than the average adult American. That lifetime will mostly consist of the painful, lingering effects of damage to joints and connective tissues, and continuing cognitive deficits (see Chapter 4).

Examples

In the 1999 steampunk western action-comedy, *The Wild, Wild West*, Will Smith's character climbs up Dr. Arliss Loveless' giant robotic spider, only to be shot point blank in the chest with a flintlock pistol. His survival of the shot is explained by his use of a chain mail vest made with 1869 technology that stops bullets, but there's no explanation of how, after the shot knocked him off the spider, he was able to survive a 5 story fall, landing on his back.

Matt Murdock in *Daredevil* is shown spitting out a broken/dislodged tooth after his first on-screen fight, and it might take less time to show how much of his body isn't scarred. His medicine cabinet is also shown to be absolutely stuffed full of painkillers like Percocet and Vicodin, suggesting that he could teach Dr. House a thing or two about living with pain.

**Rocky**

In nearly every *Rocky* film someone expresses concern about Rocky's health (in *Rocky 2* he already has trouble following his trainer's moving finger and in *Rocky 3* it's commented that his previous beatings should have killed him. In *Rocky 5* there's concern that he has sustained brain damage and might well die if he ever gets in the ring again, yet each time these health concerns and the physical toll taken on him not only mysteriously vanish by the beginning of the next movie, but the former small-time club boxer, described in the first movie by his trainer, Mickey (Burgess Merideth), as a "tomato" and a "leg breaker for some cheap second-rate loan shark," somehow becomes smarter and more sophisticated by the beginning of each movie, completely contradicting the well-known effects of repeated head trauma.

The worst offender may be *Rocky 2*. In their climactic rematch, Apollo Creed gives him twenty consecutive, unanswered shots to the face. Ouch.

# HURTING YOUR CHARACTERS

In *Rocky 4*, Drago (the cold-war, Lurch-like antagonist) says with a certain awe, "He's not human. He's like a piece of iron."

Fun fact: in that one, Dolph Lundgren actually broke a couple of Stallone's ribs. Accidentally, one would assume.

In the *Diehard* movies, John McClane fits the other, gets-badly-hurt type of action hero to a tee. In the fourth film, he takes enough damage to kill an average man 3 or 4 times, yet he still wipes out an entire assault squad occupying a building, destroys a helicopter with a police cruiser and a ramp, kills an adversary with a Ford Explorer and an elevator pit, takes out a fighter plane with an eighteen-wheeler and an elevated highway, and as a climax, shoots himself through the shoulder in order to kill the antagonist that was holding a gun against him. And all he needs after all this is to get patched up and a calm seat on the rear bumper of an ambulance. Don't mess with New York police—wow.

**Examples in literature**
Michael Crichton's *The Lost World* (1995), the sequel to *Jurassic Park*, is a prime example of this. In the book *Jurassic Park*, Ian Malcolm suffers from septicemia from a T-Rex bite and is said to be dead during a conversation near the end of the novel. At the beginning of *The Lost World*, however, he's shown giving a lecture at a university, with no explanation.

Nelson DeMille's *Plum Island*, wherein the antagonist is slashed through the abdomen, allowing his guts to spill out. This gives the protagonist enough time to pull some of the guts, place them on the antagonist's face and quip "Your guts." Later on, we find out that the antagonist survived and is on trial. Nelson DeMille fails to understand things such as blood loss, infection (as this happens in a dark, underground, abandoned barrack near a disease research facility), or the excruciating pain that would have caused the antagonist to pass out immediately. Or, he just chose to ignore them.

This trope shows up—of all places—in Georgette Heyer's classic regency romance *The Grand Sophy*. Sophy's friend is worried that her cousin might challenge him to a duel, so Sophy shoots him in the arm, then bandages him up. It's noted the injury is only a flesh wound, and blood poisoning (septicemia) isn't even mentioned.

Heroes getting shot in the shoulder is also a recurring plot point throughout her novels.

In *The Girl Who Played With Fire*, Lisbeth Salander is shot in the hip, in the back, and in the head (the last bullet getting lodged in her brain), then buried (barely) alive, yet she still manages to not only dig her way out and take revenge, but also survive all the way into and through the sequel, proving Swedish women are not to be easily dismissed.

# SIXTEEN

## TIME OF DEATH

*"No one gets out of here alive."*

—Jim Morrison, *The Doors*

"

Sometimes, in the course of writing a novel, it becomes necessary to dispose of a character. We do so with a tear in our eye knowing the sacrifice is for the greater good—or not.

Novelists are mostly a sadistic bunch. I speak with some experience here. My first book attempt, a truly terrible piece of dreck which eventually found the perfect resting place—a folder on my hard drive titled "Open for a Humility Reminder." That piece only lacked three things: good grammar, a coherent plot, and some dead bodies lying around cluttering up the otherwise tidy landscape. Which is one of the things novelists do—we kill characters.

While both we and our readers share the desire to die quietly, someplace warm, nothing could be further from what we expect from our fictional counterparts. Like most everything else in fiction, we want them to die horrible, exciting deaths that we can experience vicariously and which, is infinitely preferable to the real thing.

The question you're probably asking here (or at least I hope you're asking here) is: since this is a book about describing injuries from a subjective point of view, and we're talking about people dying, how does that work?

Except for the minor injuries we talked about in Chapter 2, most of the injuries discussed in this book can potentially result in your character's death. Hopefully, neither you nor I will need to experience most of the things already discussed in this book to be able to relate them effectively to a reader. After all, the reason for this book is to keep potential novelists from jumping off the garage roof in order to be able to adequately describe a broken bone. What we will do as creative, eloquent, individuals is what we normally do with everything else—we will do some research, use our imaginations, make our best guess, and muddle through. There is a multitude of novels that portray a character's death subjectively, but I'd be willing to bet none of those authors are writing from first-hand experience.

How you as an author choose to portray your character's death will say a lot about that character. It will also speak volumes about your integrity as an author. Readers are, generally, a perceptive lot and far more intelligent than most beginning authors give them credit for. They give us their time and their money, and all they expect in return is good grammar and an entertaining story they can use to suspend their disbelief. Doesn't seem like a lot to ask, really.

But enough philosophizing, let's kill a character or two.

When we set out to portray a character's death from a subjective point of view, we have to make an assumption: that that character's death will take enough time for them to actually become aware that they're dying. This seems like an obvious statement until we look at how a traumatic death usually works. Probably one of the best works of fiction dealing with death on an intimate level was the film *Saving Private Ryan*. From the first horrific twenty minutes on Omaha Beach, through the individual deaths of many of the characters, this is an example of some of the most engaging, emotion-evoking writing I've ever seen. Having never been in combat, I can only guess at the confusion and panic it creates, but the writing, as well as the acting, conveys those feelings exquisitely.

# HURTING YOUR CHARACTERS

Whatever genre we choose as our medium, when we kill characters, ultimately, that's the feeling we're trying to convey: confusion, because our character is experiencing something beyond his normal frame of reference, and a certain amount of panic because he's facing an unknown he has no control over. For instance, a character who's being strangled in the course of our novel will experience all of the things described in chapter 5, but at some point may realize, "I'm dying." The description of what the character does with that realization is important, and one of the things we're talking about here.

The other important thing is the common physiologic manifestations associated with death. Using that same strangled character for a minute, let's examine the physiologic steps leading to death, but let's do it in past tense the way we might in an actual novel.

"Jim's vision blurred and tunneled, going dark around the edges." This sensation is because of decreased oxygen flow to the brain. It would be expected to continue as hypoxia increases, with those dark edges taking up more and more of Jim's vision until it ultimately goes black, for him. This might best be described by something like, "The scene in front of him telescoped away to a pinpoint and disappeared along with consciousness."

Let's take it a step further and bring in the other senses.

"His mouth, fingers, and toes tingled as a feeling of calm, almost a euphoria edged around the panic." Again, these sensations are associated with hypoxia, which we would expect to increase. However, the reverse would more likely be true because as hypoxia proceeds to unconsciousness, we would expect sensory input from the body to decrease, so the tingling would probably fade away, as would the sense of euphoria as "Jim's heart rate slowed. His strength giving way to slackening as unconsciousness pushed in."

Now, that wasn't so hard, was it? Great, let's kill somebody else.

Let's try dehydration. "After the boat went down, Carol had been in the raft for the better part of two days when the headache and dizziness set in." Again, the symptoms we would normally expect with dehydration, with a gradual progression: "A little later, the dry mouth that had been her constant companion since the first day progressed to a parched, bone-dry sensation that burned the back of her throat and stuck her tongue to the roof of her mouth." Now, let's push Carol over the edge: "On the third day, the nausea progressed to cramping, and her hands and feet felt like someone was running electric current through them. Her head lolled back against the edge of the raft and she stared up at the unrelenting sun, too weak to roll over as her eyes closed for the last time."

Exit Carol, stage left.

So, in literature, death is not about death, it's about the dying. Okay, let's go for a hard one. Let's try a combination, say a bank shot, putting the nine ball in the corner pocket. Let's bump Jack, a fictional detective, off using a gunshot wound to the leg. That should be fun.

"Jack registered the bullet tearing into his thigh before he heard the roar of the gun, his leg snatched back as if by a giant hook. The bee-sting sensation was enough to get his attention, and he glanced down to see a crimson patch growing before his eyes." Again, we've injured Jack using several senses to engage the reader more fully. Next step: "He'd been shot before, but this was different. He collapsed onto the pavement with a grunt and struggled to catch his breath. He needed to get some pressure on his leg and realized with a start that he'd lost feeling below the wound. Bad sign." We've also given him a 'feeling of impending doom' as a foreshadowing to the reader, pulling them closer in anticipation of the outcome. Let's kick it up a bit. "His heart sped as he followed the blood from the rapidly-expanding pool on the pavement to the hole in the leg of his pants the size of his little finger. Not enough bleeding. Jack reached to his leg and brushed his fingertips around until he found the ping pong ball-sized hole where the bullet had exited. Beads of sweat broke out on his forehead."

The Ah-ha moment for Jack. The adrenaline surge has his heart racing. He's been through this before, and he knows how bad it is from the amount of blood he's obviously losing. Then he finds the real wound—the exit wound. Let's allow Jack to try something to help. Wanna guess whether it'll work?

"He had to get his belt off and around his leg before he passed out, and he knew he was going to pass out. The pool of blood under him was turning into a lake. He rolled onto his back and reached for his belt buckle, and the waves of pain from his leg hit like a fist. He sucked in a breath, tasting bile as he worked the leather out of the loops and around his thigh, above the wound. The dark spots that obscured his vision as he cinched the belt sparked into bright flashes when he pulled it tight. He gritted his teeth against the agony, but the blood made his fingers slippery and when he leaned his head back to catch his breath, it slipped away, loosening again. Jack dropped his head to the sidewalk and noticed he was floating on the scarlet lake now, being carried away on it like a flash flood. He had to try again. He grunted his way toward the end of his belt. It seemed a mile away as he pawed at it, kitten weak. He missed and fell back, his last thought before giving way to sleep was of Mary, of how angry she was going to be at his broken promise to always come home to her after the end of his shift and how much he loved her."

Okay, Jack, outta here. Geez. Guy took forever to cash in his chips. Guess there's just no getting rid of some people. We have a severe penetrating injury from a gunshot, emotional shock, blood loss, and loss of consciousness all playing together to paint a picture for the reader. There are as many ways to paint that picture, of course, as there are words to describe it, You might even use a sudden, unexpected death and an afterlife to show your character's death as an intermittent series of quick flashes as the character moves through the plot and her experiences bring her to the realization that she is, in fact, dead. That artistic choice is yours.

But that's the really exciting part of this artistic stuff. We get to play with the what-ifs and mix and match possibilities until we come up with something that's uniquely our own.

# Afterword

*"Be a sadist. No matter how sweet and innocent your leading characters, make awful things happen to them—that the reader may see what they're made of."*

—Kurt Vonnegut

## Superhero

All this is not to say I don't enjoy Bruce Willis walking across broken glass and then pulling a sliver the size of a small garden spade out of his foot before he runs off to battle the bad guys or shooting the antagonist through his own chest. I like a good superhero story as much as the next person, and I'm often in awe of what writers will come up with to top the last scene, but these are not realistic portrayals of what real people would experience or how they would behave, adrenaline notwithstanding. If you're writing a superhero story, well and good. Sometimes readers like an underdog to win. Try not to laugh out loud at these and other depictions you run across in your travels, though. Other members of the audience probably won't understand.

I disagree with the tenet that everything worth doing is worth doing well. I have never, to the best of my knowledge, ever washed a window well. Dishes should be done as quickly and efficiently as possible and left to their own devices to dry. When writing a book or pursuing any artistic endeavor that requires a focused mind (as almost all do), I believe people should be excused from most usual activities, with the possible exception of eating, sleeping, bathing, and toilet necessities. I would include an occasional "hello" to loved

157

ones with whom we share our lives, as they can be and often are our most loyal supporters.

There have been times in my life when, in pursuit of the perfect cut of a pane for a stained glass window or chasing the elusive brilliant opening paragraph of the novel (which I seem to have never actually found), I've been known to go without eating or sleeping for more than a full day. There've been times when I've had to be reminded that my life is not fully my own and that I've chosen to share it with a very loving and forgiving partner. Forgetting that is not a practice I recommend.

However, artistic endeavors, such as writing, art, or music, should be approached as something that is worth doing well. The arts, including writing, require diligence with regard to craft, voice, and research. And hopefully, in the process, we manage to pick up an artistic touch as well.

We all make mistakes, and I certainly make more than my fair share, but there's no excuse for authors to adopt an attitude of "no one will notice if I get it wrong." Someone almost certainly will notice and we owe our readers our best effort in making our fiction as believable and emotionally engaging as possible.

If you are reading this book, it's proof that you care. I hope I've helped you meet your goals.

# Appendix A

## WORDS TO DESCRIBE PAIN

**achy** — Adjective. Continuous, poorly localized, usually dull unpleasant sensation

**acute** — Adjective. New. Acute pain is generally any pain of immediate onset and lasting less than 3 months total. Pain lasting from 3 to 6 months is usually classified as sub-acute, and pain lasting longer than 6 months is generally considered chronic.

**agonizing** — Adjective. Very. Painful.

**angry** — Adjective. A descriptive term for a red and painful area of skin, especially pertaining to an open wound or infection.

**burning** — Adjective. Term used for describing the sensation of touching something hot, especially pertaining to muscle injuries or fevers.

**chapped** — Adjective. Dry, painful skin or lips, especially due to cold or extremely dry weather exposure.

**chronic** — Adjective. Long-lasting. Chronic pain is generally any pain lasting longer than 6 months without relief.

**constant** — Adjective. Steady. Not waxing or waning in intensity.

**crawling** — Adjective. The sensation of movement, either on or under the skin.

**crippling** — Adjective. Any pain, the intensity of which causes a generalized reduction in the function of a body part, especially an extremity.

**crushing** — Adjective. An uncomfortable sensation of pressure. Synonymous with "heavy," "vice-like," or "tight."

**dull** — Adjective. The opposite of sharp. Typically, poorly localized pain symptoms originating in the muscles, bones, or internal organs.

**excruciating** — Adjective. Extreme, unrelenting, debilitating pain.

**gnawing** — Adjective. Continuously causing pain or worry.

**griping** — Adjective. Sudden, overwhelming, debilitating pain, especially related to internal organs, and normally associated with a protective gesture of guarding, or clutching the area with one or both hands.

**heavy** — Adjective. Difficulty with movement, due to reduced strength. The feeling of decreased ability or inability to move against gravity.

**inflamed** — Adjective. Swollen, red, warm to the touch, and painful, because of injury or infection. Synonymous with "angry" or "irritated."

**intermittent** — Adjective. Waxing and waning in intensity over time. Periodic, not constant.

**irritated** — Adjective. Swollen, red, warm to the touch, and painful because of injury or infection. Synonymous with "inflamed" or "angry."

**itchy** — Adjective. An unpleasant feeling on your skin that often initiates scratching or rubbing.

**numb** — Adjective. An absence, lack of, or decrease in sensation.

**painful** — Adjective. Physical or emotional discomfort.

**piercing** — Adjective. The opposite of dull. Well localized, usually intense pain, often, but not always associated with injuries to the skin. Synonymous with "stabbing."

**pounding** — Adjective. Synonymous with pulsing, usually in time with heart rate.

**raging** — Adjective. A strong, overwhelming, or serious sensation or emotion.

**raw** — Adjective. (1) having the surface abraded or chafed (2) very irritated

**severe** — Adjective. A pain, injury, or illness is serious and unpleasant.

**sharp** — Adjective. The opposite of dull. Well localized, usually intense pain, often, but not always associated with injuries to the skin. Synonymous with "stabbing."

**shooting** — Adjective. The opposite of dull. Well localized, usually intense pain, often, but not always associated with injuries to the skin. Synonymous with "stabbing," except associated with a crescendo-decrescendo feel.

**sore** — Adjective. Painful and uncomfortable, usually as a result of an injury, infection, or too much exercise

**squeezing** — Adjective. An uncomfortable, band-like sensation of pressure. Synonymous with "vice-like" or "tight."

**stabbing** — Adjective. The opposite of dull. Well localized, usually intense pain, often, but not always associated with injuries to the skin. Synonymous with "sharp," except suddenly comes and goes.

**stiff** — Adjective. The sensation of difficulty moving to to muscular pain, especially after overuse or injury.

**stinging** — Adjective. Sharp, well localized, usually, but not always moderate pain, usually, but not always associated with injuries to the skin.

**tender** — Adjective. Painful to the touch. And objective findings consistent with subjective symptoms of pain.

**thumping** — Adjective. Synonymous with pulsing, usually in time with heart rate.

**tight** — Adjective. An uncomfortable sensation of pressure. Synonymous with "vice-like" or "squeezing." Often used to describe difficulty breathing.

**tearing** — Adjective. Extreme, prolonged, ripping or pulling sensation, either in a muscle, tendon, ligament, or skin.

**tingling** — Adjective. A slight prickling or stinging sensation, usually felt in the skin.

**unendurable** — Adjective. Unpleasant, or painful in the extreme.

**vice-like** — Adjective. An uncomfortable sensation of pressure. Synonymous with "tight" or "squeezing." Often used to describe headache-type pain.

# WORDS TO DESCRIBE SMELL, SOUND, TASTE, & TOUCH

Humans have such an advanced visual orientation that we often forget to write with our other senses. Thank goodness for the stereoscopic vision that gives (most of) us depth perception, but we so often forget to use words to describe what we smell and hear and taste. Here's a list of possibilities that you might find helpful. Notice that many of the words used to describe smell and taste overlap. This is because there is much overlap of the brain physiology involved in these two seemingly separate senses. So much so, that often a person who looses one will complain of an almost complete loss of the other.

### Smell (Olfactory)
Acidic, Acrid, Aromatic, Briny, Camphoric, Fetid, Flowery, Foul, Fragrant, Fresh, Funky, Gamy, Heady, Musky, Musty, Nasty, Noxious, Perfumed, Piney, Pungent, Rancid, Savory, Sharp, Smelly, Stinky, Stuffy, Sweet

### Taste (Gustatory)
Acidic, Biting, Bitter, Brackish, Briny, Camphoric, Dry, Flavorful, Fruity, Full-bodied, Gamy, Gross, Juicy, Peppery, Rank, Rich, Sharp, Sour, Succulent, Sugary, Sweet, Syrupy, Tangy, Tart, Zesty, Zingy

**Sound (Aural)**

Bang, Blare, Bleat, Bray, Brogue, Caterwaul, Chime, Chirp, Chortle, Chuckle, Clash, Croak, Croon, Crunch, Drone, Fizz, Grind, Groan, Gulp, Gurgle, Hoot, Howl, Jangle, Jingle, Knock, Ping, Plop, Rap, Rasp, Rattle, Roar, Rumble, Rustle, Sizzle, Slam, Slap, Slurp, Snarl, Strum, Tap, Thud, Thunk, Tinkle, Trill, Twang, Warble, Whack, Whine, Whistle, Yodel

**Touch (Tactile)**

Bristly, Burning, Cold, Cottony, Damp, Dry, Feathery, Frosty, Furry, Fuzzy, Gnarled, Hairy, Hot, Knobbed, Knotted, Leathery, Limp, Lumpy, Oily, Puffy, Ribbed, Rough, Rubbery, Sandy, Sharp, Slimy, Smooth, Sticky, Velvety, Wet

# Appendix C

## Exercises to explore ways to describe using senses other than sight

An excellent exercise that I discovered posted on the SFF World forum in June, 2007 by "hippokrene":

"The 5 x 5 x 5 x 5 x 5" method of description.

You describe the same situation/environment 5 different ways by writing 5 descriptions using all 5 senses, and you do it for 5 days a week for 5 weeks. The idea is not to make pretty prose; it's to expand the way you think and describe an environment.

Here's one situation: "He walked into a tavern."

And here's just one alternative:
Eric walked into a tavern. The smell of hickory smoke fire and cloves of garlic being roasted whole with butter created a patina over the scent of sweat and ale (1). Men chatted noisily among themselves amid the clanking of tankards on wooden tables. Dice clattered in one corner followed by a whoop of triumph from one man while others groaned (2). As Eric walked toward the back wall, sawdust crunched under his boots (3). When he reached Trevor's table, he stopped and nonchalantly lifted the glass of dark liquid (4) to his lips, and pulled a long drink of the thick, bitter liquid (5).

(The above paragraph is a condensed version of the scenario presented)

Now do this four more times. That might sound difficult at first, but think about what differences subtle changes in character sex, time period, and setting can make. For instance:

"New Year's Eve, 1941, and Germany has invaded France. A woman in an evening dress walks into a Paris bar, it's smoky and a live band played with a few people dancing. She's there to pass information to a British officer she has never met, but she has reason to believe there's a German spy waiting for her.

Or, a college football player enters a country and western bar. There's a mechanical bull, a place to dance, and a few locals looking for a fight.

It's winter, 1882, and a Victorian gentleman enters the bar of a brothel with his friends, who are going to help him with that pesky virginity.

The year is 2176, and a nano-augmented private eye enters an alien bar in order to question a crime boss about a series of murders. She's worked with the man previously, when she was a thief, and she doesn't want him to know she suspects he's involved.

Another common exercise is to take an ordinary, everyday object and describe it 5 different ways, using each sense.

I've found in my own writing that exercises like these can be very helpful in building and strengthening descriptive abilities. Have fun.

# Glossary

## SOME MEDICAL TERMS & THEIR DEFINITIONS

**A-delta nerve fibers** — Small myelinated fibers that transmit information to the brain about the emotional effects of tissue damage and pain. In acupuncture, stimulation of the A-delta system is used to inhibit pain transmission.
Jonas: Mosby's Dictionary of Complementary and Alternative Medicine. (c) 2005, Elsevier.

**Abrasion** — An excoriation, or circumscribed removal of the superficial layers of skin or mucous membrane.

**Acute pain** — Pain that is usually temporary and results from something specific, such as a surgery, an injury, or an infection.

**Afferent or sensory nerves** — Fibers that convey impulses to a ganglion or to a nerve center in the brain or spinal cord.

**Amnesia** — A disturbance in the memory of stored information of very variable durations, minutes to months, in contrast to short-term memory, manifest by total or partial inability, to recall past experiences.

Analgesia — A neurologic or pharmacologic state in which painful stimuli are moderated such that, although still perceived, they are no longer painful.

**Avulsion** — A tearing away or forcible separation.

**Baux score** — The Baux score is a system used by medical professionals to predict the chance of mortality due to a patient suffering severe burns. http://en.wikipedia.org/wiki/Baux_score

**Blood pressure** — The pressure or tension of the blood within the systemic arteries, maintained by the contraction of the left ventricle, the resistance of the arterioles and capillaries, the elasticity of the arterial walls, as well as the viscosity and volume of the blood; expressed as relative to the ambient atmospheric pressure.

**Blunt trauma** — Any injury sustained from blunt force, which may be related to MVAs/RTAs, or mishaps, falls or jumps, blows or crush injuries from animals, blunt objects or unarmed assailants. http://medical-dictionary.thefreedictionary.com/Blunt+Trauma

**C fibers (nerves)** — Unmyelinated fibers, 0.4–1.2 mcm in diameter, conducting nerve impulses at a velocity of 0.7–2.3 m/sec.

**Central Nervous System** — The brain and the spinal cord.

**Cerebral contusion** — A form of traumatic brain injury; a bruise of the brain tissue. http://en.wikipedia.org/wiki/Cerebral_contusion

**Cervical spine** — Those vertebrae immediately inferior to the skull. http://en.wikipedia.org/wiki/Cervical_vertebrae

**Choke Hold** — A general term for a grappling hold that critically reduces or prevents either air (choking) or blood (strangling) from passing through the neck of an opponent. http://en.wikipedia.org/wiki/Chokehold

**Closed (simple) fracture** — A fracture in which the broken bone does not pierce the skin Also called a closed fracture. Collins English Dictionary – Complete and Unabridged © Harper Collins Publishers 1991, 1994, 1998, 2000, 2003. http://www.thefreedictionary.com/simple+fracture

**Cognitive** — A group of mental processes that includes attention, memory, producing and understanding language, learning, reasoning, problem solving, and decision-making.

**Concussion** — A clinical syndrome usually due to head trauma, characterized by immediate but transient impairment of cerebral function, principally alteration of consciousness, but also disturbance of vision and equilibrium, without any detectable structural brain damage.

**Contusion** — Any mechanical injury (usually caused by a blow) resulting in hemorrhage beneath unbroken skin.

**Crushing Injuries** — Compression of extremities or other parts of the body that causes muscle swelling and/or neurological disturbances in the affected areas of the body, while crush syndrome is localized crush injury with systemic manifestations. http://en.wikipedia.org/wiki/Crush_syndrome

**Decompression sickness** — Term used to describe illness that results from a reduction in the ambient pressure surrounding a body. http://www.diversalertnetwork.org/medical/articles/Decompression_Illness_What_Is_It_and_What_Is_The_Treatment

**Dehydration** — 1. Deprivation of water. 2. Reduction of water content. 3. Used commonly in emergency departments to describe a state of water loss sufficient to cause intravascular volume deficits leading to orthostatic symptoms.

**Diastolic Blood pressure** — The intracardiac pressure during or resulting from diastolic relaxation of a cardiac chamber; the lowest arterial blood pressure reached during any given ventricular cycle.

**Distal** — Situated away from the center of the body, or from the point of origin; specifically applied to the extremity or distant part of a limb or organ.

**Dizziness** — Imprecise term commonly used to describe various symptoms such as faintness, giddiness, imbalance, lightheadedness, unsteadiness, or vertigo.

**Dorsal** — Of, toward, on, in, or near the back or upper surface of an organ, part, or organism.

**Dura mater** — The tough, fibrous membrane forming the outer covering of the central nervous system, consisting of periosteal and meningeal dura layer and an inner part, the dural border cell layer, continuous with the arachnoid barrier cell layer.

**Dynamic equilibrium** — A system in a steady state since forward reaction and backward reaction occur at the same rate. http://www.biology-online.org/dictionary/Dynamic_equilibrium

**Efferent or motor neurons** — Otherwise known as motor or effector neurons, carry nerve impulses away from the central nervous system to effectors such as muscles or glands (and also the ciliated cells of the inner ear). http://en.wikipedia.org/wiki/Efferent_nerve_fiber

**Endocrine system** — The system of glands, each of which secrets different types of hormones directly into the bloodstream (some of which are transported along nerve tracts) to regulate the body. http://en.wikipedia.org/wiki/Endocrine_system

**Enzymes** — A macromolecule that acts as a catalyst to induce chemical changes in other substances, while itself remaining apparently unchanged by the process.

**Epidural** — On (or outside) the dura mater. [Usage note: epidural and extradural are nearly synonymous, with the exception that epidural implies immediate proximity to the dura mater, and extradural may be unconnected with it.]

**Excoriation** — A scratch mark; a linear break in the skin surface, usually covered with blood or serous crusts.

**Explosive Decompression** — The term uncontrolled decompression here refers to the unplanned depressurization of vessels that are occupied by people. For example, an aircraft cabin at high altitude, a spacecraft, or a hyperbaric chamber. http://en.wikipedia.org/wiki/Uncontrolled_decompression

**Fainting game** — Refers to intentionally cutting off oxygen to the brain with the goal of inducing temporary syncope and euphoria. http://en.wikipedia.org/wiki/Choking_game

**Fracture** — A break, especially the breaking of a bone or cartilage.

**Heat Exhaustion** — A form of reaction to heat, marked by prostration, weakness, and collapse, resulting from severe dehydration.

**Heat Stroke** — A severe and often fatal illness produced by exposure to excessively high temperatures, especially when accompanied by marked exertion; characterized by headache, vertigo, confusion, hot dry skin, and a slight rise in body temperature; in severe cases, high fever, vascular collapse, and coma develop.

**Hematoma** — A localized mass of extravasated blood that is relatively or completely confined within an organ or tissue, a space, or a potential space; the blood is usually clotted (or partly clotted), and, depending on its duration, may manifest various degrees of organization and decolorization.

**Hemoglobin** — The red protein of erythrocytes, consisting of approximately

3.8% heme and 96.2% globin, which as oxyhemoglobin, transports oxygen from the lungs to the tissues where the oxygen is readily released.

**Homeostasis** — The state of equilibrium (balance between opposing pressures) in the body with respect to various functions and to the chemical compositions of the fluids and tissues.
2. The processes through which such bodily equilibrium is maintained.

**Hypothalamus** — About the size of a pearl, the hypothalamus directs a multitude of important functions in the body. It is the control center for many autonomic functions of the peripheral nervous system. Connections with structures of the endocrine and nervous systems enable the hypothalamus to play a vital role in maintaining homeostasis. For example, blood vessel connections between the hypothalamus and pituitary gland allow hypothalamic hormones to control pituitary hormone secretion. As a limbic system structure, the hypothalamus also influences various emotional responses. http://biology.about.com/od/anatomy/p/Hypothalamus.htm

**Hypovolemia** — A decreased amount of blood in the body

**Incision** — A cut; a surgical wound; a division of the body parts, usually made with a knife.

**Ion** — An atom or molecule in which the total number of electrons is not equal to the total number of protons, giving the atom a net positive or negative electrical charge. http://en.wikipedia.org/wiki/Ion

**Laceration** — A torn or jagged wound, or an accidental cut wound.

**Lancinating** — Denoting a sharp cutting or tearing pain.

**Ligature** — Refers to strangling with some form of cord such as rope, wire, or shoe laces, either partially or fully encircling the neck. http://en.wikipedia.org/wiki/Strangling#Ligature_strangulation

**Limbic system** — A set of evolutionarily primitive brain structures located on top of the brainstem and buried under the cortex. Limbic system structures are involved in many of our emotions and motivations, particularly those that are related to survival.
http://biology.about.com/od/anatomy/a/aa042205a.htm

**Lumbosacral spine** — The five vertebrae between the rib cage and the pelvis. They are the largest segments of the vertebral column and are characterized by the absence of the foramen transversarium within the transverse process, and by the absence of facets on the sides of the body.
http://en.wikipedia.org/wiki/Lumbar_vertebrae

**Mammalian diving reflex** — A reflex in mammals which optimizes respiration to allow staying underwater for extended periods of time. It is exhibited strongly in aquatic mammals (seals, otters, dolphins, etc.), but exists in a weaker version in other mammals, including humans.
http://en.wikipedia.org/wiki/Mammalian_diving_reflex

**Minor Injuries** — Any injury unlikely to be dangerous to life or health.

**Modulation** — A relatively new concept wherein several classes of neurotransmitters regulate diverse populations of central nervous system neurons, in contrast to direct synaptic transmission, in which one presynaptic neuron directly influences a postsynaptic partner.

**Moxibustion** — in Eastern medicine, the burning of moxa (a downy substance obtained from the dried leaves of an Asian plant related to mugwort) on or near a person's skin as a counterirritant (heat or an ointment used to produce surface irritation of the skin, thereby counteracting underlying pain or discomfort).

**Myelin** — The lipoproteinaceous material, composed of regularly alternating membranes of lipid lamellae (cholesterol, phospholipids, sphingolipids, and phosphatidates) and protein, of the myelin sheath.

**Nervous system** — The part of an animal's body that coordinates the actions of the animal and transmits signals between different parts of its body. In most types of animals it consists of two main parts, the central nervous system (CNS) and the peripheral nervous system (PNS). http://en.wikipedia.org/wiki/Nervous_system

**Neuron** — The morphologic and functional unit of the nervous system, consisting of the nerve cell body, the dendrites, and the axon.

**Nitrogen narcosis** — 1. Narcosis produced by nitrogenous materials such as occurs in certain forms of uremia and hepatic coma;
2. Stuporous condition characterized by disorientation and by loss of judgment and skill, attributed to an increased partial pressure of nitrogen in the inspired air of deep-sea divers during underwater operations. Commonly referred to as "rapture of the deep."

**Nociception** — the sensory nervous system's response to certain harmful or potentially harmful stimuli. In nociception, intense chemical (e.g., chili powder in the eyes), mechanical (e.g., cutting, crushing), or thermal (heat and cold) stimulation of sensory nerve cells called nociceptors produces a signal that travels along a chain of nerve fibers via the spinal cord to the brain. Nociception triggers a variety of physiological and behavioral responses and usually results in a subjective experience of pain in sentient beings.

**Open (compound) fracture** — An open fracture is a broken bone that penetrates the skin. http://orthopedics.about.com/cs/brokenbones/g/openfracture.htm

**Oxygen toxicity** — 1. A bodily disturbance resulting from breathing high partial pressures of oxygen; characterized by visual and hearing abnormalities, unusual fatigue while breathing, muscular twitching, anxiety, confusion, incoordination, and convulsions; can occur when excessive quantities of oxygen are administered in patients (such as during adult respiratory distress syndrome), resulting in worsening of pulmonary infiltrates and clinical deterioration; although the mechanism for development of the condition is obscure, a disruption of enzymatic activity is likely, perhaps as a result of free radical formation.

2. Exposure of the lungs to greater than 60% oxygen for periods exceeding 24–48 hours can lead to severe, irreversible pulmonary fibrosis.

**Pain receptors** — A sensory receptor that responds to potentially damaging stimuli by sending nerve signals to the spinal cord and brain. This process, called nociception, usually causes the perception of pain. Nociceptors were discovered by Charles Scott Sherrington in 1906. http://en.wikipedia.org/wiki/Nociceptor

**Perception** — The organization, identification and interpretation of sensory information in order to represent and understand the environment. http://en.wikipedia.org/wiki/Perception

**Peripheral Nervous System** — The peripheral part of the nervous system external to the brain and spinal cord from their roots to their peripheral terminations. This includes the ganglia, both sensory and autonomic, and any plexuses through which the nerve fibers and all the peripheral nerves run.

**pH** — A measure of the activity of the (solvated) hydrogen ion. p[H], which measures the hydrogen ion concentration is closely related to, and is often written as, pH. Pure water has a pH very close to 7 at 25°C. Solutions with a pH less than 7 are said to be acidic and solutions with a pH greater than 7 are basic or alkaline. http://en.wikipedia.org/wiki/PH

**Physiology** — The science concerned with the normal vital processes of animal and vegetable organisms, especially as to how things normally function in the living organism rather than to their anatomic structure, their biochemical composition, or how they are affected by drugs or disease.

**Plasma** — The proteinaceous fluid (noncellular) portion of the circulating blood, as distinguished from the serum obtained after coagulation.

**Proximal** — Nearer to a point of reference such as an origin, a point of attachment, or the midline of the body.

**Pulse** — Rhythmic dilation of an artery, produced by the increased volume of blood thrown into the vessel by the contraction of the heart. A pulse may also at times occur in a vein or a vascular organ, such as the liver.

**Puncture wound** — A wound in which the opening is relatively small compared with the depth, as produced by a narrow pointed object.

**Receptor** — 1. an organ or cell able to respond to light, heat, or other external stimulus and transmit a signal to a sensory nerve.
2. a region of tissue, or a molecule in a cell membrane, that responds specifically to a particular neurotransmitter, hormone, antigen, or other substance.

**Shock** — The condition in which the cells of the body receive inadequate amounts of oxygen secondary to changes in perfusion

**Somatic structures** — Supplies and receives neurons to and from the skin, skeletal muscles, joints and tendons.
http://people.eku.edu/ritchisong/301notes2b.html

**Spinal cord** — The elongated cylindric portion of the cerebrospinal axis, or central nervous system, which is contained in the spinal or vertebral canal.

**Sprain** — An injury to a ligament as a result of abnormal or excessive forces applied to a joint, but without dislocation or fracture.

**Strain** — To injure by over stretching, stretching too fast, or overexertion (usually refers to a muscle tear).

**Strangulation** — Depriving of air, usually by forcible means. The act or condition of being strangled, in any sense: compression, constriction, herniation of an intestine through an opening in the abdominal musculature.

**Subdural space** — An artificial or potential space created by the separation of the dura mater and the arachnoid mater, usually due to trauma, as in subdural hematoma.

**Systolic Blood pressure** — The maximum pressure exerted by contraction of the heart during each heartbeat.

**Thermal conduction** — The transfer of heat energy by microscopic diffusion and collisions or quasi-particles within a body due to a temperature gradient.

**Thoracic spine** — Those vertebrae that also carry a pair of ribs, and lie caudal to the cervical vertebrae. http://en.wikipedia.org/wiki/Thoracic_vertebrae

**Total body surface area (TBSA)** — An assessment measure of burns of the skin. In adults, the "rule of nines" is used to determine the total percentage of area burned for each major section of the body. In some cases, the burns may cover more than one body part, or may not fully cover such a part; in these cases, burns are measured by using the casualty's palm as a reference point for 1% of the body. http://en.wikipedia.org/wiki/Total_body_surface_area

**Transduction** — Stimulus alerting events wherein a mechanical/physical/etc stimulus is converted into an action potential which is transmitted along axons towards the central nervous system where it is integrated. http://en.wikipedia.org/wiki/Transduction_(physiology)

**Transmission** — The chemical process by which signaling molecules called neurotransmitters are released by a neuron (the presynaptic neuron), and bind to and activate the receptors of another neuron (the postsynaptic neuron).

**Vena cava** — The(superior) vena cava is a large diameter, short, vein that carries deoxygenated blood from the upper half of the body to the heart's right atrium. The (Inferior) vena cava is the large vein that carries deoxygenated blood from the lower half of the body to the right atrium.

**Vertigo** — A sensation of spinning or whirling motion. Vertigo implies a definite sensation of rotation of the subject (subjective vertigo) or of objects about the subject (objective vertigo) in any plane.

**Ventral** — Relating to or situated on or close to the anterior aspect of the human body or the lower surface of the body of a nonhuman animal.

**Visceral structures** — Smooth muscle, cardiac muscle, and glands. The visceral motor fibers make up the autonomic nervous system, which has two divisions: the parasympathetic division for controlling of normal body functions, e.g. the normal operation of the digestive system, and the sympathetic, also known as fight or flight, division; which is important in helping cope with stress. http://people.eku.edu/ritchisong/301notes2b.html

# Bibliography

No book is ever written in a vacuum, and whatever stars we strain to reach, we are always standing on the shoulders of those who came before us. This book is certainly no exception. As you can see from the list included, I've used extensive references to literature, films, television, medical texts and, that phenomenon of the 21st century, Wikipedia. For the benefit of those who wish to further their own understanding of the topic, I've made every attempt to cite the references I used in writing this book, and give those dedicated individuals their due. And I attempted to do so while maintaining the integrity of what I believe was each original author's intent. I thank all of them for their commitment and additions to humanity's knowledge.

Further thoughts on Wikipedia: traditionally, Wikipedia has been ignored and chastised as a reference source for intellectual articles. My personal feeling is that this denigration is unfounded and prejudicial, as Wikipedia is both alive in that it is constantly evolving and improving and completely open to peer review. I believe (perhaps wrongly so) that this prejudice is based, at least in part on the traditional intellectual snobbery attached to textbook publication. My hope is that as we as a culture progress and accept digital forms of information transmission, we will, likewise, accept this source as the valuable and convenient reference source that it is. As with all things truly democratic, there are occasional bumps in its road, but this should serve as a reminder to all of us to take nothing at face value, but instead, remain skeptical and verify references. The reader should also be aware that my personal bias is for the free (as in both unobstructed and low-to-no-cost) sharing of information. I plan to donate a portion of any proceeds from the sale of this book to Wikipedia for its continued maintenance and improvement.

1. Blood loss symptoms —
https://www.google.com/#hl=en&tbo=d&biw=1774&bih=850&sclient=psy-ab&q=blood+loss+symptoms&oq=blood+loss+symptoms&gs_l=hp.3..0i7l4.16427.18510.2.19017.10.10.0.0.0.2.162.1114.4j6.10.0.les%3B..0.0...1c.1.ImAvlJNF5_I&pbx=1&bav=on.2,or.r_gc.r_pw.r_cp.r_qf.&fp=9ea53e6e32d8ec62&bpcl=38093640
2. Hypovolemia — http://en.wikipedia.org/wiki/Hypovolemia
3. Humerus fracture —
http://www.nlm.nih.gov/medlineplus/ency/article/000167.htm
4. Internal bleeding causes, symptoms, signs and diagnoses —
http://en.wikipedia.org/wiki/Hypovolemia
5. Hypovolemic shock —
http://www.nlm.nih.gov/medlineplus/ency/article/000167.htm
6. Three Kings (1999 film) —
http://en.wikipedia.org/wiki/Three_Kings_(1999_film)
7. Playing God (1997 film) —
http://en.wikipedia.org/wiki/Playing_God_(film)
8. Blunt chest trauma — http://emedicine.medscape.com/article/428723-overview#a30
9. Vasovagal response — http://en.wikipedia.org/wiki/Vasovagal_response
10. Stages of shock — http://www.wisegeek.com/what-are-the-stages-of-shock.htm#lbss
11. Biological response to psychic trauma —
http://www.cirp.org/library/psych/vanderkolk2/
12. Traumatic amputation —
http://en.wikipedia.org/wiki/Traumatic_amputation
13. Blunt trauma — http://www.scribd.com/doc/106135828/Blunt-Trauma
14. Explosion — http://en.wikipedia.org/wiki/Explosion
15. Burns — http://www.nlm.nih.gov/medlineplus/burns.html
16. Burns — http://en.wikipedia.org/wiki/Burn
17. Burns — http://www.nigms.nih.gov/Education/Factsheet_Burns.htm
18. Burns: Symptoms - Mayo Clinic —

http://www.mayoclinic.com/health/burns/DS01176/DSECTION=symptoms

19. Heat exhaustion — http://www.mayoclinic.com/health/heat-exhaustion/DS01046

20. Cold injuries — http://www.hypothermia.org/Hypothermia_Ed_pdf/Alaska-Cold-Injuries.pdf

21. Frostbite — http://www.umm.edu/altmed/articles/frostbite-000065.htm

22. Frostbite: symptoms — http://www.mayoclinic.com/health/frostbite/DS01164/DSECTION=symptoms

23. Spinal cord injury — http://en.wikipedia.org/wiki/Spinal_cord_injury

24. Avulsion injury — http://en.wikipedia.org/wiki/Avulsion_injury

25. Excoriation — http://www.wisegeek.com/what-is-an-excoriation.htm

26. Hematoma — http://en.wikipedia.org/wiki/Hematoma

27. Bruise — http://en.wikipedia.org/wiki/Bruise

28. Puncture wounds — http://www.ncemi.org/cse/cse1015.htm

29. Cuts and puncture wounds — http://health.nytimes.com/health/guides/injury/cuts-and-puncture-wounds/overview.html

30. Avulsion injury — http://en.wikipedia.org/wiki/Avulsion_injury

31. Lacerations, causes, & symptoms — http://www.injuryinformation.com/injuries/lacerations.php

32. Injuries — http://forensicpathologyonline.com/index.php?option=com_content&view=category&id=50&layout=blog&Itemid=76

33. Words to describe smell, sound, taste, touch — http://acreativemoment.com/2008/07/18/resources/words-to-describe-smell-sound-taste-touch/

34. Explosive decompression and vacuum exposure — http://www.geoffreylandis.com/vacuum.html

35. List of signs and symptoms of diving disorders — http://en.wikipedia.org/wiki/List_of_signs_and_symptoms_of_diving_disorders

36. Nurse to Nurse Trauma Care by Donna Nayduch - https://docs.google.com/viewer?a=v&q=cache:cxDKq1SgLVUJ:www.mhprofessional.com/downloads/products/0071596771/nayduch_ch01.pdf+&hl=en&g

l=us&pid=bl&srcid=ADGEESh3aSg-
qWBK5fHcV4KLykO3fk8VMmNgmfUqlEfbNc8f1PAPBuScs1W5k9xuW8s
1juv2Ieu8xKHC5bmNIabL8YGFM_CIo2lWvN71grMxfv1wC7Yw6CNdjZ
7ttRGGblMKp3he_3NR&sig=AHIEtbTLnFXAOKJ5RCEUXrGHL3z9Klqk
Lg

37. Pathology and Mechanisms of TBI by Jeffrey T Barth & Frank G. Hillary
— http://schatz.sju.edu/neuro/patho/pathophysiology.html

38. Head Injury Mechanisms —
http://www.eurailsafe.net/subsites/operas/HTML/Section3/Page3.3.1.2.htm

40. Concussion — http://en.wikipedia.org/wiki/Concussion

41. Hard to Kill (film plot) — http://en.wikipedia.org/wiki/Hard_to_Kill

42. Rocky (film plot) — http://en.wikipedia.org/wiki/Rocky

43. Rocky (film series overview) —
http://en.wikipedia.org/wiki/Rocky_(film_series)

44. James Bond (film series overview) —
http://en.wikipedia.org/wiki/List_of_James_Bond_films

45. A Knight's Tale (film plot) —
http://en.wikipedia.org/wiki/A_Knight%27s_Tale

46. Daredevil (film plot) — http://en.wikipedia.org/wiki/Daredevil_(film)

47. Die Hard (film series) —
http://en.wikipedia.org/wiki/Die_Hard_(franchise)

48. Peripheral nervous system —
http://en.wikipedia.org/wiki/Peripheral_nervous_system

49. Gray's anatomy of the human body —
http://education.yahoo.com/reference/gray/

50. The portrayal of coma in contemporary motion pictures. Wijdicks, EF,
Wijdicks, CA. Neurology May 9, 2006 vol. 66 no. 9, 1300-1303.

51. Head-Lines, 2011 Creative Writing Anthology, Matthew Colbeck, ed.

52. Studies of the Stephanie Plum Books —
http://gary.appenzeller.net/PlumStudies2.html#Injuries

53. Electric shock — http://en.wikipedia.org/wiki/Electric_shock

54. Head Trauma and Coma — Waking Is Rising And Dreaming Is Sinking:
The Search For Identity In Coma Literature, by Matthew Colbeck, PhD

# Index

## A

## B

## C

www.ingramcontent.com/pod-product-compliance
Lightning Source LLC
Chambersburg PA
CBHW062147280526
45788CB00001B/338